The SQL standard
A complete reference

The SQL standard

A complete reference

Rick F. van der Lans
Shell Netherlands International

Translated by
Andrea Gray

Prentice Hall

Academic Service

First published in English in 1989 by
Prentice Hall International (UK) Ltd
66 Wood Lane End, Hemel Hempstead
Hertfordshire, HP2 4RG
A division of
Simon & Schuster International Group
and
Academic Service, Schoonhoven, Holland

A co-publication between Prentice Hall International (UK) Ltd
and Academic Service, Schoonhoven

© 1989 Academic Service and Prentice Hall International (UK) Ltd

Original Dutch language edition published by
Academic Service, Schoonhoven

© 1988 Academic Service

Printed and bound in Great Britain by
BPCC Wheatons Ltd, Exeter

Library of Congress Cataloging-in-Publication Data

Lans, Rick F. van der.
The SQL standard.

Translated from the Dutch.
Bibliography: p.
Includes index.
1. SQL (Computer program language). I. Title.
QA76.73.S67L37   1988   005.75'6   88-35752
ISBN 0-13-840059-8

British Library Cataloguing-in-Publication Data

Lans, Rick F. van der
The SQL standard: a complete reference
1. Relational machine readable files.
Searching. Programming languages : SQL
I. Title
005.75'6

ISBN 0-13-840059-8

---

1 2 3 4 5   93 92 91 90 89

ISBN 0-13-840059-8

Contents

Preface

Around 1983 the development of a standard for the relational database language, SQL, (Structured Query Language), was begun under the auspices of the ISO (International Standards Organisation). The standard was completed in 1986.

This book is completely devoted to the official *SQL standard*. It is not intended as a textbook, rather as a reference. To clarify statements, I have often included illustrative examples.

At the moment there are differences between the SQL standard and existing SQL implementations such as DB2, ORACLE and SQL/DS. Most implementations have more statements than the SQL standard. Therefore, in this book I describe a number of SQL statements which do not appear in the standard, but are defined in most SQL implementations. (The next version of the SQL standard will most probably include some of these statements.) In order to avoid misunderstandings I have described these statements in a separate chapter.

Some of you will be acquainted with my *Introduction to SQL* and are possibly asking yourself how it relates to this book. You should regard this book about the SQL standard as complementary to the *Introduction to SQL*. In my first book I 'taught' the SQL language, whereas this book is intended primarily as a reference work.

For whom is this book intended?

This book is intended for the following two groups:

- Those who, in writing SQL programs, must comply with the standard. If programs are written according to the standard they can be migrated from one SQL environment (which meets the criteria of the standard) to another.

- Those who have to learn SQL and want to know how the standard is defined.

This reference can be used in conjunction with existing course materials for SQL courses.

Prerequisite knowledge

Readers should have knowledge of SQL. If you are not familiar with the SQL language then I advise you to read *Introduction to SQL*. *The SQL Standard: a Complete Reference* leads on from *Introduction to SQL*.

And finally ...

I would like to use this preface to thank various people for their contributions to this book. I am greatly indebted to Corine Cools, Marianne Scheerens, Dirk-Jan Kooijman and Stephen Cannan for their useful criticism and advice. The latter two are members of the Netherlands work group which is engaged in the development of the SQL standard. I want to thank Andrea Gray for the way in which she has translated this book. Last, I am grateful to Diane Cools for her support and motivation.

I would like to ask readers to send me comments, criticisms and suggestions concerning the book. Please send them to the publisher marked Attention: Rick F. van der Lans, *The SQL Standard: a Complete Reference*. Many thanks in anticipation of your cooperation.

Rick F. van der Lans
Alphen aan den Rijn, 16 March 1989

Chapter 1

Introduction to the SQL standard

Introductory remark: When we speak of *SQL* in this book we mean the *SQL standard*. When we are discussing a commercial implementation of SQL we will mention it explicitly.

1.1   The history and status of the SQL standard

The SQL standard has been developed by workgroup WG3 of TC97/SC21 of the ISO (International Standards Organisation). WG3 is concerned principally with projects in the area of database languages.

The ANSI (American National Standards Institute) began the development of a standard for relational database languages. In 1982 they conducted a study of the possibilities offered by the then available relational database management systems. The results of these studies are summarized in [SCHM83]. At that stage it was not the intention to define a special standard for SQL. Rather, the original objective was the development of a standard for relational database languages.

The initial concept of a standard was based on a document written by IBM. The database language SQL was defined in this document, which became accepted as the basis of the eventual standard. For this reason the objective was also altered and became the development of a standard for SQL. Therefore, the title of the final report is not: *Relational Database Language*, but *Database Language SQL*.

In 1986 the SQL standard was completed and described in the document *ISO 9075 Database Language SQL*; see [ISO87a]. The SQL standard consists of two levels and has one addendum: *ISO 9075 Addendum 1 Integrity Enhancements*; see [ISO87b].

At the end of 1986 when the SQL standard had been completed, people immediately began working on the successor: *SQL2*; see [ISO88]. In this book we will refer to it as the SQL2 standard. We expect that the SQL2 standard will be completed in 1990. SQL will probably be extended in the following four areas:

- statements for specifying other sorts of integrity rules
- statements for changing the structure of tables
- improved possibilities for data manipulation
- inclusion of embedded SQL in the standard

The aims of developing this new standard are:

- To extend the set of statements in the SQL standard so as to gain a head start over the suppliers. In this way the direction of their product development can be influenced.

- To make SQL more complete, more consistent and more in line with the principles of the relational model. SQL, as it is defined in the standard, still contains a number of undesirable constructions; see among others [DATE87].

1.2 Three sorts of SQL statements

The SQL statements are divided into three language groups:

- **Data Definition Language (DDL):** These statements are used to define database structures, integrity rules and users' privileges (for example CREATE TABLE and CREATE VIEW).

- **Data Manipulation Language (DML):** DML statements are used to update or query data (for example UPDATE and SELECT).

- **Module Language:** Module language statements are declared DML statements which can be called and executed from within a program (written in a programming language).

Note: The standard contains only statements which are concerned with the logical database structure. Statements for creating indexes and databasespaces, for example, are not included.

1.2.1 DDL statements

The SQL standard recognizes the following DDL statements:

- CREATE SCHEMA
- CREATE TABLE
- CREATE VIEW
- GRANT

In the SQL standard each table and view belongs to a so-called *schema*. When the schema is created all tables, views and authorities are also established and the name of a user is specified. This user is the only owner of the schema, and, at the same time, of all the tables and views belonging to the schema. Each user has a maximum of one schema. A database can consist of multiple schemas.

Note: The SQL standard includes no statement for deleting tables and for adding columns to existing tables. Most SQL implementations do have statements for these functions, such as the DROP TABLE statement. We will undoubtedly see most of these statements included in the new SQL2 standard; see [ISO88].

1.2.2 DML statements

For manipulating data SQL recognizes two sorts of DML statements: cursor *dependent* and cursor *independent*. The cursor dependent statements are:

- DECLARE
- OPEN
- FETCH
- CLOSE
- DELETE
- UPDATE

A cursor is a mechanism whereby the result of a 'search' condition — consisting of a collection of rows — can be read row by row. A cursor must be named for each statement.

The cursor independent DML statements are:

- SELECT
- INSERT
- UPDATE
- DELETE
- COMMIT
- ROLLBACK

These statements process and directly access the contents of tables without the intervention of cursors. The major difference between cursor dependent and cursor independent statements is that the former processes individual rows and the latter a set of rows.

Note: Two forms of the UPDATE and the DELETE statement exist. For that reason they appear in both groups of DML statements.

1.2.3 Module language statements

The SQL standard recognizes the following module language statements:

- MODULE
- PROCEDURE

You can use DML statements in two ways:

- included in a module
- included in a program written in another programming language (known as *embedded SQL*).

An *(SQL) module* is a collection of *(SQL) procedures*. Each procedure contains one DML statement. By linking a program written in another programming language to a module, DML statements which have been defined in procedures can be called and activated from the program. How this link between program and module is realized is not described in the standard. When the procedures are invoked, users can supply parameters. Thus, a program itself contains no DML statements. There is a maximum of one module per program, and a module is suitable for only one programming language.

Note: At the time of writing, there were no SQL implementations which allowed for modules and procedures.

The second way to use DML statements is directly inserted in a program, without the medium of modules. We call this *embedded SQL*. This form of SQL, however, is not part of the standard, but is described in separate annexes. We discuss embedded SQL in Chapter 5.

1.3 Support of the SQL standard

The number of commercial implementations of SQL is increasing rapidly. In [DATE87] Chris Date noted that there were already more than fifty systems supporting SQL. Unfortunately, we have to point out that although these systems are called SQL by their respective suppliers, they are all different from one another.

The most important advantage of a standard is that there is one, clear, unambiguous description of SQL. In this way the differences between the various SQL implementations will gradually disappear. This will have a positive effect on the general acceptance and widespread usage of SQL.

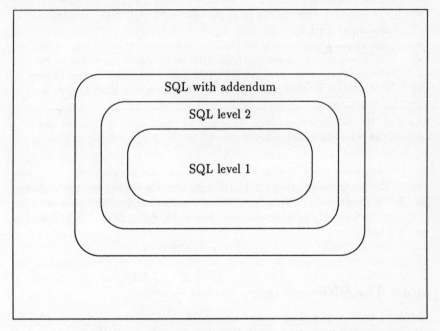

Figure 1.1: **Two levels of SQL and the addendum**

A commercial SQL implementation conforms to the SQL standard when each statement conforms to the syntax of the standard and executes according to the rules of the standard. This does not mean, however, that an SQL implementation cannot contain additional statements.

In order to make it easier for some suppliers to meet the standard's requirements, its authors defined two levels. Level 2 contains *all* SQL statements and specifications. We describe level 2 in this book. Level 1 is the same as level 2 minus a number of specifications. In Chapter 6 we cover those specifications which do not appear in level 1. SQL level 1 is, therefore, a subset of SQL level 2. This means that whenever suppliers claim that their product supports the SQL standard they must indicate which level.

As well as the two levels there is also an addendum which details other extensions to the standard. All these extensions have to do with the specification of integrity rules. In Figure 1.1 we show the relationship between the two SQL levels and the addendum pictorially.

If a supplier claims that his product supports the SQL standard, he must say to what degree this is so. There are six possibilities:

- The product implements all SQL DDL and SQL DML statements according to level 1.
- The product implements all SQL DDL and SQL DML statements according to level 2.
- The product implements all SQL DDL statements according to level 1.
- The product implements all SQL DDL statements according to level 2.
- The product implements all SQL DML statements according to level 1.
- The product implements all SQL DML statements according to level 2.

As well, the supplier must indicate which of the following facilities are supported; at least one is necessary.

- The product can process SQL DML statements interactively.
- The product can process SQL DML statements via the module language.
- The product can process SQL DML statements embedded in one ore more of the following programming languages: COBOL, FORTRAN, Pascal or PL/I.

1.4   The BNF notation

We use a variation of the so-called *Backus Naur Form* (BNF) for the formal presentation of the syntax of the SQL statements. This is named after John Backus and Peter Naur. The meanings of the metasymbols we use are the same as those for the symbols in the SQL standard.

BNF adopts a language of so-called *substitution rules* or *production rules* consisting of a series of symbols. One *symbol* is defined in each production rule. A symbol can be an SQL statement, a table name or a semi-colon, for example. The *terminal symbol* is a special type of symbol. Examples of terminal symbols are the word CLOSE and the colon. All symbols, apart from terminal symbols, are defined in terms of other symbols in a production rule.

You can compare a production rule with the definition of an element whose definition uses elements which are, in turn, defined somewhere else. An element corresponds in this case to a symbol.

The following metasymbols do not form part of the SQL language, but belong to the notation.

< >   Non-terminal symbols are given in < >. For each non-terminal symbol there exists a production rule. We will give the names of non-terminal symbols in lower case letters. The `<select statement>` and the `<table name>` are two examples of non-terminal symbols.

::=   This symbol is used in a production rule to separate the non-terminal symbol which is defined (left) from the definition (right). The ::= symbol should be read as 'is defined as'. We show below the production rule for the CLOSE statement as an example:

```
<close statement> ::= CLOSE <cursor name>
```

Explanation: The CLOSE statement consists, then, of the terminal symbol 'CLOSE' followed by the non-terminal symbol cursor name. There should also be a production rule for `<cursor name>`.

| Alternatives are shown with the | symbol. Our example below shows the production rule for the element `<programming language>`:

```
<programming language> ::= COBOL | FORTRAN | PASCAL | PLI
```

[ ]   Whatever is placed between square brackets, [and], *may* be used. Here we show the production rule for the table reference:

```
<table reference> ::=
    <table name> [ <correlation name> ]
```

Explanation: A table reference always consists of a table name which may optionally be followed by a correlation name.

...   The ellipsis shows what may be repeated one or more times. Below is the production rule for an unsigned integer:

```
<unsigned integer> ::= <digit>...
```

Explanation: An unsigned integer consists of a series of digits (minimum of one).

{ }   All symbols between braces together form a group. For example, braces are used with the | symbol to show precisely what the alternatives are. Our example here is the production rule for the FROM clause:

```
<from clause> ::=
    FROM <table reference> [ { , <table reference> }... ]
```

Explanation: A FROM clause begins with the terminal symbol 'FROM' and is followed by a table reference. It is possible to follow this table reference with a list of elements, where each element consists of a comma followed by a table reference.

Additional remarks:

- Whatever is presented in upper case letters, as well as the symbols which are not part of the formal syntax (but belong to the notation) must be adopted unaltered.

- The sequence of the symbols in the right hand side of the production rule is fixed.

1.5 The structure of the book

Chapter 2, *The sports club sample database*, describes a database used by all the examples. This database forms the basis of the competition administration in a sports club.

Chapter 3, *Common elements*, contains the definitions of the various common elements used to construct DML and DDL statements.

Chapter 4, *Definitions of the SQL statements*, covers the syntax, the description and examples of usage of each SQL statement.

Chapter 5, *Embedded SQL*, describes how SQL can be embedded in a program written in another language. This form of SQL is not included in the standard but *is* described in its annexes.

Chapter 6, *Two levels of the SQL standard*, discusses the differences between the two levels on which the SQL standard has been built. We name all the specifications which do not appear in level 1.

Chapter 7, *Addendum 1: Integrity enhancements*, describes how integrity rules can be specified.

Chapter 8, *Definitions of additional SQL statements*, gives the syntax, description and examples of SQL statements which do *not* form part of the SQL standard, but *are* implemented in many commercial versions of SQL.

The book closes with three appendices and an index. Appendix A contains the reserved words of SQL. Appendix B contains as a reference the definitions of all the SQL statements. Appendix C is a bibliography.

Chapter 2

The sports club sample database

This chapter describes a database that could be used by a sports club to administer its participation in the competition series. All the examples in this book are based on this database so you should study it carefully if you are not already familiar with it.

Note: This sample database has been borrowed from [LANS88].

2.1 Description of the sports club database

The database comprises four tables:

- PLAYERS
- TEAMS
- GAMES
- PENALTIES

The PLAYERS table contains data about members of the club. It contains no historical data. If a player renounces his or her membership then he or she disappears from the table. In the case of moving house, as well, the old address is over-written with a new address. In other words, the old address is not retained anywhere. Two players cannot have the same name and initials.

The sports club has two types of members: *recreational players* and *competition players*. The first group play games only among themselves (that is, no games against players from other clubs). The results of these friendly games are not recorded. Competition players play in teams against other clubs and these results are recorded. Each player, regardless of whether he or she plays competitively, has a unique number. This player number is assigned by the club. Each competition player must also be registered with the sports league and this organization gives each player a unique league number. If a competition player no longer plays matches but becomes a recreation player, his or her league number is deleted. Therefore recreation players have no league number but do have a player number.

The club has a number of teams that take part in the competition. The division in which each team competes at any given time is recorded. Again, no historical data is kept in this table. If a team is promoted or demoted to another division, then the record is simply over-written with new information. The same goes for the captain of the team; when a new captain is appointed the number of the former captain is over-written.

A team consists of four players. During a game each player plays against one member of the opposing team. A team does not always consist of the same people and reserves are sometimes needed when players are sick or on holiday. A player either wins or loses a match; a draw is not possible. In the GAMES table we show how many matches a particular player for a particular team has won and lost. This table *does* contain historical data. At the beginning of a season the number of won and lost matches are not set to zero but counted up and brought forward. Thus a player can appear in the GAMES table more than once, but each time it must be for a different team. It is not possible from this table to deduce the composition of a particular team.

If a player is badly behaved (arrives late, behaves aggressively or does not turn up at all) then the league imposes a penalty in the form of a fine. The club pays these fines and records them in the PENALTIES table. As long as a player continues to play competitively the record of his or her penalties remains in this table.

If a player leaves the club, all his or her data from the four tables is destroyed. If a club withdraws a team, all data for that team is removed from the TEAMS and GAMES tables.

Below we give a description of the columns in each of the four tables.

PLAYERS	
PLAYERNO	Unique number of the player
NAME	Surname of the player, without initials
INITIALS	Initials of the player; no full stops or spaces are used after each separate letter
YEAR_OF_BIRTH	Year in which the player was born
SEX	Sex of the player: M(ale) or F(emale)
YEAR_JOINED	Year in which the player joined the club
STREET	Name of the street in which the player lives
HOUSENO	Number of the house
POSTCODE	Postcode
TOWN	Town or city in which the player lives
PHONENO	Area code followed by a hyphen and then subscriber's telephone number
LEAGUENO	League number which is assigned by the league, or a dash for recreational players

TEAMS	
TEAMNO	Unique number of the team
PLAYERNO	The player number of the team captain
DIVISION	The division in which the league has placed the team

GAMES	
TEAMNO	Number of the team
PLAYERNO	Number of the player
WON	Number of games that the player has won for this team
LOST	Number of games that the player has lost for this team

PENALTIES	
PAYMENTNO	Unique number of each penalty the club must pay
PLAYERNO	Number of the player who has incurred the penalty
DATE	Date on which the penalty is received and paid
AMOUNT	Amount of the penalty

2.2 The structure of the database

Logical relationships exist between the tables; for example each player number in the PENALTIES table must appear in the GAMES table. Such a relationship is called a *foreign key*. These relationships are shown schematically in Figure 2.1 (not all columns are included). An arrow under a column (or combination of columns) indicates a *primary key*. An arrow from one table to another represents a foreign key.

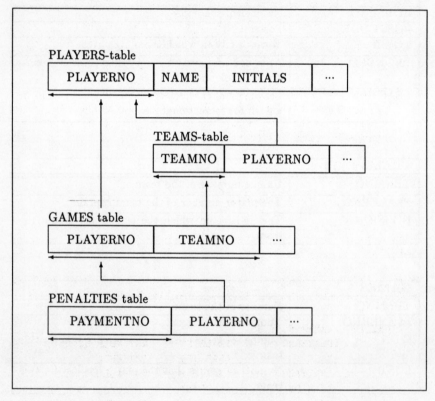

Figure 2.1: **Schematic version of the sports club sample database**

Explanation of the foreign keys:

- **From TEAMS to PLAYERS:** Each captain of a team is, of course, a player. The set of player numbers from the TEAMS table is a subset of the set of player numbers from the PLAYERS table.

- **From GAMES to PLAYERS:** Each player who competes for a particular team must appear in the PLAYERS table. The set of player numbers from the GAMES table is a subset of the set of player numbers from the PLAYERS table.

- **From GAMES to TEAMS:** Each team that appears in the GAMES table must also be present in the TEAMS table, because a player can only compete for registered teams. The set of team numbers from the GAMES table is a subset of the set of team numbers from the TEAMS table.

- **From PENALTIES to GAMES:** A penalty can only be imposed on players who have participated in the competition. The set of player numbers from the PENALTIES table is a subset of the set of player numbers from the GAMES table.

2.3   The database schema

Below we show the schema of the sports club sample database and the associated tables.

Note: In Chapter 7 we return to this schema and add the additional specifications which the addendum to the SQL standard recognizes.

```
CREATE    TABLE PLAYERS
          (PLAYERNO        SMALLINT        NOT NULL UNIQUE,
          NAME             CHAR(15)        NOT NULL,
          INITIALS         CHAR(3)         NOT NULL,
          YEAR_OF_BIRTH    SMALLINT                ,
          SEX              CHAR(1)         NOT NULL,
          YEAR_JOINED      SMALLINT        NOT NULL,
          STREET           CHAR(15)        NOT NULL,
          HOUSENO          CHAR(4)                 ,
          POSTCODE         CHAR(6)                 ,
          TOWN             CHAR(10)        NOT NULL,
          PHONENO          CHAR(10)                ,
          LEAGUENO         CHAR(4)                 ,
          UNIQUE (NAME, INITIALS))
```

```
CREATE    TABLE TEAMS
          (TEAMNO          SMALLINT     NOT NULL UNIQUE,
          PLAYERNO         SMALLINT     NOT NULL,
          DIVISION         CHAR(6)      NOT NULL)


CREATE    TABLE GAMES
          (TEAMNO          SMALLINT     NOT NULL,
          PLAYERNO         SMALLINT     NOT NULL,
          WON              SMALLINT     NOT NULL,
          LOST             SMALLINT     NOT NULL,
          UNIQUE (TEAMNO, PLAYERNO))


CREATE    TABLE PENALTIES
          (PAYMENTNO       INTEGER      NOT NULL UNIQUE,
          PLAYERNO         SMALLINT     NOT NULL,
          DATE             CHAR(6)      NOT NULL,
          AMOUNT           DECIMAL(7,2) NOT NULL)
```

2.4   The contents of the tables

We show the contents of the tables below. All our examples assume that these are the table contents.

The PLAYERS table:

PLAYERNO	NAME	INITIALS	YEAR OF BIRTH	SEX	YEAR JOINED	STREET	...
6	Parmenter	R	1964	M	1977	Haseltine Lane	...
44	Baker	E	1963	M	1980	Lewis Street	...
83	Hope	PK	1956	M	1982	Magdalene Road	...
2	Everett	R	1948	M	1975	Stoney Road	...
27	Collins	DD	1964	F	1983	Long Drive	...
104	Moorman	D	1970	F	1984	Stout Street	...
7	Wise	GWS	1963	M	1981	Edgecombe Way	...
57	Brown	M	1971	M	1985	Edgecombe Way	...
39	Bishop	D	1956	M	1980	Eaton Square	...
112	Bailey	IP	1963	F	1984	Vixen Road	...
8	Newcastle	B	1962	F	1980	Station Road	...
100	Parmenter	P	1963	M	1979	Haseltine Lane	...
28	Collins	C	1963	F	1983	Old Main Road	...
95	Miller	P	1934	M	1972	High Street	...

PLAYERNO	...	HOUSENO	POSTCODE	TOWN	PHONENO	LEAGUENO
6	...	80	1234KK	Stratford	070-476573	8467
44	...	23	4444LJ	Inglewood	064-368753	1124
83	...	16a	1812UP	Stratford	070-353548	1608
2	...	43	3575NH	Stratford	070-237893	2411
27	...	804	8457DK	Eltham	079-234857	2513
104	...	65	9437AO	Eltham	079-987571	7060
7	...	39	9758VB	Stratford	070-347689	-
57	...	16	4377CB	Stratford	070-473458	6409
39	...	78	9629CD	Stratford	070-393435	-
112	...	8	6392LK	Plymouth	060-548745	1319
8	...	4	6584WO	Inglewood	064-458458	2983
100	...	80	1234KK	Stratford	070-476573	6524
28	...	10	1294QK	Midhurst	072-659599	-
95	...	33a	5746OP	Douglas	075-867564	-

The TEAMS table:

TEAMNO	PLAYERNO	DIVISION
1	6	first
2	27	second

The GAMES table:

TEAMNO	PLAYERNO	WON	LOST
1	6	9	1
1	44	7	5
1	83	3	3
1	2	4	8
1	57	5	0
1	8	0	1
2	27	11	2
2	104	8	4
2	112	4	8
2	8	4	4

The PENALTIES table:

PAYMENTNO	PLAYERNO	DATE	AMOUNT
1	6	801208	100.00
2	44	810505	75.00
3	27	830910	100.00
4	104	841208	50.00
5	44	801208	25.00
6	8	801208	25.00
7	44	821230	30.00
8	27	841112	75.00

Chapter 3

Common elements

SQL statements use a number of common elements. Below we define and illustrate the following elements:

* character
* column specification
* data type
* literal
* name
* predicate
* query expression
* query specification
* search condition
* set function specification
* subquery
* table expression
* table name
* value expression
* value specification

We have arranged the common elements in alphabetical order. For each element we give:

* a description (what the purpose of the element is and where it is used)
* the format; sometimes we also repeat definitions of other common elements in order to clarify the format
* additional rules which are not included in the BNF, but are concerned with the syntax of SQL
* general rules which have to do with the meaning of common elements
* examples

3.1 Character

Description

A character is a terminal symbol of SQL and part of a character string literal.

Format

```
<character> ::=
   <digit> | <letter> | <special character>

<digit> ::=
   0 | 1 | 2 | 3 | 4 | 5 | 6 | 7 | 8 | 9

<letter> ::=
   <lower case letter> | <upper case letter>

<lower case letter> ::=
   a | b | c | d | e | f | g | h | i | j |
   k | l | m | n | o | p | q | r | s | t |
   u | v | w | x | y | z

<upper case letter> ::=
   A | B | C | D | E | F | G | H | I | J |
   K | L | M | N | O | P | Q | R | S | T |
   U | V | W | X | Y | Z

<special character> ::= see Additional rule 1
```

Additional rules

1. The special characters are all character representations which are not digits or letters. The per cent sign (%) and the underscore (_) belong to the set of special symbols. Each supplier is free to implement other special symbols.

3.2 Column specification

Description

A column specification defines a column in a table. Columns are uniquely identified by the combination of the name of the column and the identification of the table in which the column belongs.

Format

```
<column specification> ::=
   <column name> |
   <table name>.<column name> |
   <correlation name>.<column name>

<table name> ::=
   [ <authorization identifier>. ] <table identifier>
```

Additional rules

1. In order to indicate precisely which column is meant in a column specification, a table name must be given before the column name.
    In the following statement a table name is placed before each PLAYERNO column otherwise it would not be clear which column was intended.

    ```
    SELECT   DISTINCT NAME, INITIALS
    FROM     PLAYERS, PENALTIES
    WHERE    PLAYERS.PLAYERNO = PENALTIES.PLAYERNO
    ```

2. A correlation name is an alternative name for a table name. Correlation names are defined in the FROM clause.
    A correlation name is necessary in the following statement because the PLAYERS table is referenced twice in the FROM clause.

    ```
    SELECT   B.PLAYERNO
    FROM     PLAYERS A, PLAYERS B
    WHERE    A.YEAR_OF_BIRTH < B.YEAR_OF_BIRTH
    AND      A.PLAYERNO = 27
    ```

3.3 Data type

Description

A data type is a description of a set of values with equivalent, distinctive properties. A value can be a NULL value. Data types are used in CREATE TABLE statements, among others, to indicate the type of the column values.

Format

```
<data type> ::=
   CHARACTER [ ( <length> ) ] |
   CHAR      [ ( <length> ) ] |
   NUMERIC   [ ( <precision> [,<scale>] ) ] |
   DECIMAL   [ ( <precision> [,<scale>] ) ] |
   DEC       [ ( <precision> [,<scale>] ) ] |
   INTEGER   |
   INT       |
   SMALLINT  |
   FLOAT     [ ( <precision> ) ] |
   REAL      |
   DOUBLE PRECISION

<length> ::= <unsigned integer>

<precision> ::= <unsigned integer>

<scale> ::= <unsigned integer>
```

Additional rules

1. CHAR is a synonyn for CHARACTER.

2. DEC is a synonym for DECIMAL.

3. INT is a synonym for INTEGER.

4. Length and precision must be greater than zero.

5. If the length of the CHARACTER data type is omitted, SQL assumes a length of 1 position.

6. If the scale of the data types NUMERIC and DECIMAL are omitted, SQL assumes a scale of 0.

---

7. For the data types NUMERIC and DECIMAL the scale may not be greater than the precision.

8. With NUMERIC an exact numeric data type is specified with a precision equal to the specified precision and a scale equal to the specified scale.

9. With DECIMAL an exact numeric data type is specified with a scale equal to the specified scale and whose precision equals or is greater than the specified precision. The difference between DECIMAL and NUMERIC is that the actual precision for DECIMAL is dependent on the supplier whereas for NUMERIC it is not.

10. With INTEGER an exact numeric data type integer is specified with a precision which is dependent on the supplier and with a scale of zero.

11. With SMALLINT an exact numeric data type is specified with a precision which is supplier dependent and not greater than the precision of the INTEGER data type and with a scale of zero.

12. With FLOAT an approximate numeric data type is specified with a binary precision equal to or greater than the specified precision.

13. With REAL an approximate numeric data type is specified whose precision is supplier dependent.

14. With DOUBLE PRECISION an approximate numeric data type is specified with a supplier dependent precision which is greater than the supplier dependent precision of the REAL data type.

Examples

```
CHARACTER
CHAR(4)
NUMERIC(7,2)
DECIMAL(6)
DEC(4,0)
FLOAT(8)
```

3.4 Literal

Description

A literal is any not NULL value. Literals are used principally in DML statements. In INSERT statements, for example, they are used to specify values in a new row, and in SELECT statements to form search conditions.

Format

```
<literal> ::=
   <character string literal> |
   <numeric literal>

<character string literal> ::=
   '<character representation>...'

<character representation> ::= <character> | ''

<numeric literal> ::=
   <exact numeric literal> | <approximate numeric literal>

<exact numeric literal> ::=
   [ + | - ] <unsigned integer> [ .<unsigned integer> ] |
   [ + | - ] <unsigned integer>. |
   [ + | - ] .<unsigned integer>

<unsigned integer> ::= <digit>...

<approximate numeric literal> ::= <mantissa>E<exponent>

<mantissa> ::= <exact numeric literal>

<exponent> ::= [ + | - ] <digit>...
```

Additional rules

1. A character representation is any character apart from quotation marks.

2. Every double quotation mark within a character string literal represents a single quotation mark.

3.   The value of an approximate numeric literal is equal to:

   mantissa $\times \ 10^{exponent}$

Examples

Correct numeric literals are:

```
     38
    +12
    -.7
  -14E5
  +2456.
```

Correct character string literals are:

```
'Jim'
'''tis'
'1234'
''''
```

The following INSERT statement uses three literals; two numeric (3 and 100) and one character string ('third').

```
INSERT INTO  TEAMS
        (TEAMNO, PLAYERNO, DIVISION)
VALUES (3, 100, 'third')
```

3.5 Name

Description

Names are identifiers for, among other things, tables, columns, parameters and views.

Format

```
<correlation name>         ::= <identifier>
<cursor name>              ::= <identifier>
<authorization identifier> ::= <identifier>
<column name>              ::= <identifier>
<module name>             ::= <identifier>
<table identifier>         ::= <identifier>
<parameter name>          ::= <identifier>
<procedure name>          ::= <identifier>

<identifier> ::=
   <upper case letter>
   [ { [ _ ] { <upper case letter> | <digit> } }... ]
```

Additional rules

1. A name can be up to 18 positions long.

2. A name may not be the same as any of the reserved words, see Appendix A.

Examples

The following names are correct:

```
PLAYERS    YEAR_OF_BIRTH    A123_ABC
```

3.6 Predicate

Description

Predicates are used in search conditions. The value of a predicate is true, false or unknown.

Format

```
<predicate> ::=
   <value expression> <comparison operator> <value expression> |
   <value expression> <comparison operator> <subquery> |
   <value expression> [ NOT ] BETWEEN <value expression>
      AND <value expression> |
   <value expression> [ NOT ] IN
      ( <value specification> {,<value specification>}... ) |
   <value expression> [ NOT ] IN <subquery> |
   <column specification> [ NOT ] LIKE <pattern>
      [ ESCAPE <escape character> ] |
   <column specification> IS [ NOT ] NULL |
   <value expression> <comparison operator> ALL <subquery> |
   <value expression> <comparison operator> ANY <subquery> |
   <value expression> <comparison operator> SOME <subquery> |
   EXISTS <subquery>

<comparison operator> ::=
   = | <> | < | > | <= | >=

<pattern> ::= <value specification>

<escape character> ::= <value specification>
```

Additional rules

1. The data types of expressions compared in a predicate must be comparable. All numeric data types are comparable with one another, as are all alphanumeric data types.

2. The data type of the value specification of a pattern and an escape character is alphanumeric.

3. The data type of the escape character is alphanumeric and has a length of one position.

General rules

1. Two alphanumeric values are equal when all the character representations in the same ordinal position are equal. Note that the lower case letter a is not equal to the upper case letter A.

2. The search condition 'x BETWEEN y AND z' is equivalent to 'x >= y AND x <= z'.

3. The search condition 'x IN (u, v, w)' is equivalent to 'x = u OR x = v OR x = w'.

4. The search condition 'x IN S' is equivalent to 'x =ANY S'.

5. The search condition 'x NOT IN S' is equivalent to 'x <>ALL S'.

6. The search condition 'x IS NULL' is true, when x is equal to the NULL value.

7. When no escape character is specified with the LIKE operator the per cent sign (%) stands for zero or more possible character representations and the underscore (_) for exactly one character representation.

8. SOME is a synonym for ANY.

9. Suppose that θ is an arbitrarily chosen comparison operator, that S is a subquery and that $s_1, s_2, \ldots, s_n$ are the values of the result of S. It follows that 'x θ ANY(S)' is equivalent to 'x θ s_1 OR x θ s_2 OR ...OR x θ s_n'.

10. Suppose that θ is an arbitrarily chosen comparison operator, that S is a subquery and that $s_1, s_2, \ldots, s_n$ are the values of the result of S. It follows that 'x θ ALL(S)' is equivalent to 'x θ s_1 AND x θ s_2 AND ...AND x θ s_n'.

11. The search condition 'EXISTS S' is true, when the result of the subquery S is *not* empty.

12. The meanings of the comparison operators are:

operator	meaning
=	equal to
<>	not equal to
<	less than
>	greater than
<=	less than or equal to
>=	greater than or equal to

Examples

Give the players who joined the club more than twenty years after they were born.

```
SELECT    *
FROM      PLAYERS
WHERE     YEAR_OF_BIRTH + 20 < YEAR_JOINED
```

Give the male players who were born after 1970.

```
SELECT    *
FROM      PLAYERS
WHERE     SEX = 'M' AND YEAR_OF_BIRTH > 70
```

Give the players who have a league number.

```
SELECT    *
FROM      PLAYERS
WHERE     LEAGUENO IS NOT NULL
```

Or:

```
SELECT    *
FROM      PLAYERS
WHERE     LEAGUENO = LEAGUENO
```

Give the players who were born in the period 1962–1967.

```
SELECT   *
FROM     PLAYERS
WHERE    YEAR_OF_BIRTH BETWEEN 1962 AND 1967
```

Give the players who were born in Stratford or Plymouth.

```
SELECT   *
FROM     PLAYERS
WHERE    TOWN IN ('Stratford', 'Plymouth')
```

Give the players whose name begins with the upper case letter B.

```
SELECT   *
FROM     PLAYERS
WHERE    NAME LIKE 'B%'
```

Give the players whose street name contains an underscore.

```
SELECT   *
FROM     PLAYERS
WHERE    STREET LIKE '%#_%' ESCAPE '#'
```

Give the players who have incurred at least one penalty.

```
SELECT   *
FROM     PLAYERS
WHERE    PLAYERNO IN
         (SELECT   PLAYERNO
          FROM     PENALTIES)
```

Give the oldest players.

```
SELECT   *
FROM     PLAYERS
WHERE    YEAR_OF_BIRTH <= ALL
         (SELECT   YEAR_OF_BIRTH
          FROM     PLAYERS)
```

Give the players who do not belong in the group of oldest players.

```
SELECT   *
FROM     PLAYERS
WHERE    YEAR_OF_BIRTH > ANY
         (SELECT   YEAR_OF_BIRTH
          FROM     PLAYERS)
```

Give the players who have incurred no penalties.

```
SELECT   *
FROM     PLAYERS
WHERE    NOT EXISTS
         (SELECT   *
          FROM     PENALTIES
          WHERE     PENALTIES.PLAYERNO = PLAYERS.PLAYERNO)
```

3.7   Query expression

Description

A query expression is constructed from a set of query specifications. The result of a query expression is the same as the UNION of the results of the individual query specifications. Query expressions are used in DECLARE CURSOR statements.

Format

```
<query expression> ::=
   <query term> |
   <query expression> UNION [ ALL ] <query term>

<query term> ::=
   <query specification> | ( <query expression> )

<query specification> ::=
   SELECT [ ALL | DISTINCT ] <select list>
   <table expression>

<select list> ::=
   <value expression> [ {,<value expression>}... ] | *

<table expression> ::=
   <from clause>
   [ <where clause> ]
   [ <group by clause> ]
   [ <having clause> ]
```

Additional rules

1.   If UNION is used the following conditions apply:

   • the number of value expressions in each select list must be the same;

   • you may use only an '*' or a series of column specifications in the select list;

   • the data types of the value expressions to which the UNION applies must be the same.

General rules

1. Use of UNION *without ALL* in a cursor declaration causes redundant
    duplicate rows to be deleted. By adding ALL these duplicate rows are
    kept.

Examples

Give the player numbers of those who have incurred at least one penalty.

```
SELECT    DISTINCT PLAYERNO
FROM      PENALTIES
```

Give the player number and town of all players who live in Stratford.

```
SELECT    PLAYERNO, TOWN
FROM      PLAYERS
WHERE     TOWN = 'Stratford'
```

Give a list of the games which have been won and lost, retaining the duplicate
rows.

```
SELECT    WON
FROM      GAMES
UNION     ALL
SELECT    LOST
FROM      GAMES
```

3.8   Query specification

Description

A query specification is used in query expressions, definitions of cursors, views and INSERT statements.

Format

```
<query specification> ::=
   SELECT [ ALL | DISTINCT ] <select list>
   <table expression>

<select list> ::=
   <value expression> [ {,<value expression>}... ] | *

<table expression> ::=
   <from clause>
   [ <where clause> ]
   [ <group by clause> ]
   [ <having clause> ]

<from clause> ::=
   FROM <table reference> [ {,<table reference>}... ]

<where clause> ::=
   WHERE <search condition>

<group by clause> ::=
   GROUP BY <column specification>
            [ {,<column specification>}... ]

<having clause> ::=
   HAVING <search condition>

<table reference> ::=
   <table name> [ <correlation name> ]
```

Additional rules

1. A query specification is only valid if the user has the SELECT privilege on all tables which are named in it.

2. If a view (with a GROUP BY clause) is specified in the FROM clause then the other three clauses may *not* be used. In that case, also, the FROM clause may consist of only one table reference.
   Given the following view:

   ```
   CREATE    VIEW INHABITANTS (TOWN, NUMBER) AS
   SELECT    TOWN, COUNT(*)
   FROM      PLAYERS
   GROUP BY TOWN
   ```

   The following query specification is *correct*:

   ```
   SELECT    *
   FROM      INHABITANTS
   WHERE     TOWN IN ('Stratford', 'Plymouth')
   ```

   The query specification below, however, is *incorrect*, because the FROM clause contains a grouped view as well another table name:

   ```
   SELECT    PLAYERS.PLAYERNO
   FROM      INHABITANTS, PLAYERS
   WHERE     INHABITANTS.TOWN = PLAYERS.TOWN
   AND       INHABITANTS.TOWN IN ('Stratford', 'Plymouth')
   ```

3. When the table expression contains a GROUP BY clause, each value expression in the select list *or* a column specification must be what appears in the GROUP BY clause *or* a set function specification.
   The following query specification is *incorrect*, because the TOWN column does not occur in the GROUP BY clause.

   ```
   SELECT    TOWN
   FROM      PLAYERS
   GROUP BY PLAYERNO
   ```

4. When the table expression contains *no* GROUP BY clause and when the select list contains a set function specification, each column specification must be placed in a set function specification.
   The following query specification is *incorrect* because the SELECT clause contains a set function specification (COUNT(*)) and at the same time a column specification (TOWN) has been named which is not within a set function specification.

   ```
   SELECT    TOWN, COUNT(*)
   FROM      PLAYERS
   ```

5. When a query specification forms part of the definition of a view or a cursor, you must know whether the query specification may be updated or not. If it *is* the case, then the view or cursor concerned may also be updated. A query specification is updatable when:

- the word DISTINCT is not used
- each value expression in the select list is a column specification
- only one table is referenced in the FROM clause
- the WHERE clause in the table expression contains no subqueries
- the table expression contains no GROUP BY clause

General rules

1. The use of DISTINCT causes all redundant duplicate rows to be deleted.

Examples

The following query specifications are updatable:

```
SELECT   *
FROM     PLAYERS
WHERE    PLAYERNO = 27


SELECT   TEAMNO, PLAYERNO
FROM     GAMES
WHERE    PLAYERNO > 100
AND      WON = LOST - 5
```

The following four query specifications are *not* updatable:

```
SELECT   PLAYERNO + 14
FROM     PLAYERS


SELECT   PLAYERS.PLAYERNO, NAME, INITIALS
FROM     PLAYERS, PENALTIES
WHERE    PLAYERS.PLAYERNO = PENALTIES.PLAYERNO


SELECT   PLAYERNO, NAME, INITIALS
FROM     PLAYERS
WHERE    PLAYERNO IN
         (SELECT   PLAYERNO
          FROM     PENALTIES)
```

```
SELECT    TOWN, COUNT(*)
FROM      PLAYERS
GROUP BY TOWN
```

3.9   Search Condition

Description

Search conditions are used in such statements as SELECT, UPDATE, DE-
LETE and INSERT. A search condition defines which rows must be included
in a result or which rows must be processed.

Format

```
<search condition> ::=
   <boolean term> |
   <search condition> OR <boolean term>


<boolean term> ::=
   <boolean factor> |
   <boolean term> AND <boolean factor>


<boolean factor> ::=
   [ NOT ] <boolean primary>


<boolean primary> ::=
   <predicate> | ( <search condition> )


<predicate> ::=
   <value expression> <comparison operator> <value expression> |
   <value expression> <comparison operator> <subquery> |
   <value expression> [ NOT ] BETWEEN <value expression>
      AND <value expression> |
   <value expression> [ NOT ] IN
      ( <value specification> {,<value specification>}... ) |
   <value expression> [ NOT ] IN <subquery> |
   <column specification> [ NOT ] LIKE <pattern>
      [ ESCAPE <escape-character> ] |
   <column specification> IS [ NOT ] NULL |
   <value expression> <comparison operator> ALL <subquery> |
   <value expression> <comparison operator> ANY <subquery> |
   <value expression> <comparison operator> SOME <subquery> |
   EXISTS <subquery>
```

General rules

The truth table below gives for two search conditions, A and B, all possible values with AND, OR and NOT.

A	B	A AND B	A OR B	NOT A
true	true	true	true	false
true	false	false	true	false
true	unknown	unknown	true	false
false	true	false	true	true
false	false	false	false	true
false	unknown	false	unknown	true
unknown	true	unknown	true	unknown
unknown	false	false	unknown	unknown
unknown	unknown	unknown	unknown	unknown

3.10   Set function specification

Description

Functions are used to perform statistical calculations on sets of values or sets of rows.

Format

```
<set function specification> ::=
   COUNT(*) |
   <distinct set function> |
   <all set function>

<distinct set function> ::=
   { AVG | MAX | MIN | SUM | COUNT }
     ( DISTINCT <column specification> )

<all set function> ::=
   { AVG | MAX | MIN | SUM } ( [ ALL ] <value expression> )
```

Additional rules

1.   No other set functions may be used within a set function. The construction AVG(MIN(PLAYERNO)) is, therefore, *incorrect*.

2.   The result of COUNT(*) has a numeric data type with a scale of zero.

3.   The set functions SUM and AVG can be used only in numeric expressions.

General rules

1.   The result of a distinct set function is achieved by first deleting all NULL values and then duplicate values.

2.   The result of an all set function is achieved by deleting all NULL values.

3.   Omission of the words DISTINCT and ALL is equivalent to specifying ALL.

4.   COUNT(*) presents the number of rows which form the result.

5.   The set functions AVG, MAX, MIN and SUM have the NULL value as a result when the column specification concerned contains no values.

6.   The MAX and MIN set functions determine the highest and lowest values respectively. The data type of these set functions is dependent on the data types of the value expression of the column specification.

7.   The SUM set function is used to calculate the sum of all values.

8.   The AVG set function calculates the arithmetic mean of all values.

Examples

The following set of values occur in the (fictitious) column NUMBER:

```
1, 2, 3, 4, 1, 4, 4, NULL, 5
```

Below we show examples of the values of a number of set function specifications:

```
MIN(NUMBER)              ==> 1
MAX(NUMBER)              ==> 5
MAX(ALL NUMBER)          ==> 5
SUM(NUMBER)              ==> 24
AVG(NUMBER)              ==> 3
COUNT(DISTINCT NUMBER)   ==> 5
MIN(DISTINCT NUMBER)     ==> 1
MAX(DISTINCT NUMBER)     ==> 5
SUM(DISTINCT NUMBER)     ==> 15
AVG(DISTINCT NUMBER)     ==> 3
COUNT(*)                 ==> 9
```

How many penalties are there and what is the highest amount?

```
SELECT   COUNT(*), MAX(AMOUNT)
FROM     PENALTIES
```

How many penalties are equal to the lowest penalty?

```
SELECT   COUNT(*)
FROM     PENALTIES
WHERE    AMOUNT =
         (SELECT   MIN(AMOUNT)
          FROM     PENALTIES)
```

Give the number of each player who has incurred more than one penalty.

```
SELECT    PLAYERNO
FROM      PENALTIES
GROUP BY  PLAYERNO
HAVING    COUNT(*) > 1
```

3.11   Subquery

Description

Subqueries can be used only in search conditions to select rows.

Format

```
<subquery> ::=
   ( SELECT [ ALL | DISTINCT ] { <value expression> | * }
   <table expression> )

<table expression> ::=
   <from clause>
   [ <where clause> ]
   [ <group by clause> ]
   [ <having clause> ]

<from clause> ::=
   FROM <table reference> [ {,<table reference>}... ]

<where clause> ::=
   WHERE <search condition>

<group by clause> ::=
   GROUP BY <column specification>
            [ {,<column specification>}... ]

<having clause> ::=
   HAVING <search condition>

<table reference> ::=
   <table name> [ <correlation name> ]
```

Additional rules

1. A subquery is valid only if the user has the SELECT privilege on all
    tables named in it.

2. If the subquery is *not* used with EXISTS the result of it must consist of
    one value expression.
    The following subquery is *incorrect* because the select list in the subquery

---

consists of two value expressions, while the subquery is not used with EXISTS.

```
SELECT   *
FROM     PLAYERS
WHERE    TOWN IN
         (SELECT   TOWN, STREET
          FROM     PLAYERS
          WHERE    PLAYERNO = 27)
```

3. In cases where the subquery occurs after a comparison operator in the search condition, the result of the subquery must consist of one row. The following subquery is *incorrect*, then, because the subquery returns more than one row, while a comparison operator occurs in the search condition.

```
SELECT   *
FROM     PLAYERS
WHERE    YEAR_OF_BIRTH =
         (SELECT   YEAR_OF_BIRTH
          FROM     PLAYERS)
```

4. When the table expression in the FROM clause contains a grouped view, *no* set function specifications may appear in the value expression.

5. When the table expression contains a GROUP BY clause, each value expression in the select list, or a column specification, must also occur in the GROUP BY clause or a set function specification.

6. When the table expression contains *no* GROUP BY clause and when the select list contains a set function specification, each column specification must be within a set function specification.

Examples

Give the name of each player who has played at least one game for the first team.

```
SELECT   NAME
FROM     PLAYERS
WHERE    PLAYERNO IN
         (SELECT   PLAYERNO
          FROM     GAMES
          WHERE    TEAMNO = 1)
```

Give the number of each team for whom player 57 has *not* played.

```
SELECT    TEAMNO
FROM      TEAMS
WHERE     NOT EXISTS
          (SELECT    *
          FROM       GAMES
          WHERE      PLAYERNO = 57
          AND        TEAMNO = TEAMS.TEAMNO)
```

3.12 Table expression

Description

Table expressions form the common link between subqueries and query specifications.

Format

```
<table expression> ::=
   <from clause>
   [ <where clause> ]
   [ <group by clause> ]
   [ <having clause> ]

<from clause> ::=
   FROM <table reference> [ {,<table reference>}... ]

<where clause> ::=
   WHERE <search condition>

<group by clause> ::=
   GROUP BY <column specification>
            [ {,<column specification>}... ]

<having clause> ::=
   HAVING <search condition>

<table reference> ::=
   <table name> [ <correlation name> ]
```

Additional rules

1. The same two table names may not occur in the FROM clause unless both are followed by a correlation name.

2. If a view (containing a GROUP BY) is specified in the FROM clause, the other three clauses may not be used and the FROM clause must name a single table reference.

3. The same correlation name may not occur in the list of table references in a FROM clause.

4. *No* set function specifications may appear in the search condition of a WHERE clause. Function specifications may only be specified in the search condition of a HAVING clause.

5. NULL values are regarded by the GROUP BY clause as equal values and are presented in one group.

6. All column specifications which appear in a HAVING clause must be columns on which grouping has been performed or those which are named in a set function specification.

General rules

1. When the table expression has *no* GROUP BY, but does have a HAVING clause, there is only one group and no column on which it has been grouped.

Examples

See, among others, query expression, query specification and subquery.

3.13   Table name

Description

Tables are identified uniquely by the combination of the name of the owner and the table identifier. The owner is the one whose name is specified in the schema to which the table belongs.

Format

```
<table name> ::=
   [ <authorization identifier>. ] <table identifier>
```

Additional rules

1.   The authorization identifier *must* be specified when the table being queried or updated does not belong to the schema of the user processing the statement.

Examples

Show the entire contents of the PLAYERS table created by John.

```
SELECT   *
FROM     JOHN.PLAYERS
```

3.14 Value expression

Description

A value expression represents a numeric or a character string value.

Format

```
<value expression> ::=
   <term> |
   <value expression> + <term> |
   <value expression> - <term>

<term> ::=
   <factor> |
   <term> * <factor> |
   <term> / <factor>

<factor> ::=
   [ + | - ] <primary>

<primary> ::=
   <value specification> |
   <column specification> |
   <set function specification> |
   ( <value expression> )
```

Additional rules

1. A value expression, constructed from a set function specification, may not contain operaters such as *, /, + or -.

2. If the data type of a primary is alphanumeric, then the value expression may not contain operators. The data type of the result of the value expression is also alphanumeric.

3. If the data types of two operands are unsigned integer, then the data type of the result is also an unsigned integer. If s_1 and s_2 are the respective scales of the first and second operands, then the scale of the result is:

- for addition or subtraction, the greater of s_1 and s_2
- for multiplication, the result of $s_1 + s_2$
- for division, it is supplier dependent

4. If one of the two operands is an approximate numeric literal, then the data type of the result is also an approximate numeric literal.

General rules

1. If the value of one of the primaries in a value expression equals the NULL value, then the result of the total value expression is the NULL value.

2. The precision and the scale of the result of a value expression where an unsigned integer is used is supplier dependent.

3. In calculating the value of a value expression you assume the following priorities: 1) from left to right, 2) brackets, 3) multiplication and division, 4) addition and subtraction

4. The meanings of the operators are:

operator	meaning
*	multiplication
/	division
+	addition
−	subtraction

Examples

```
(YEAR_OF_BIRTH - 1900) * 20
WON + LOST
AVG(YEAR_OF_BIRTH)
```

3.15   Value specification

Description

A value specification allows you, for example, to pass to a SELECT statement
a value which does *not* occur in a table. Examples include values of parameters
and variables.

Format

```
<value specification> ::=
   <parameter specification> |
   <variable specification> |
   <literal> |
   <system variable>

<parameter specification> ::=
   <parameter name> [ [ INDICATOR ] <parameter name> ]

<variable specification> ::=
   <variable name> [ [ INDICATOR ] <variable name> ]

<literal> :=
   <character string literal> |
   <numeric literal>

<system variable> ::= USER
```

Additional rules

1.   The data type of a parameter used as an indicator must be defined as
     NUMERIC and have a scale of zero.

2.   The data type of a variable used as an indicator is supplier dependent.

3.   A parameter specification can only be used in a module.

4.   A variable specification can only be used in an embedded SQL statement.

5.   The data type of the system variable USER is alphanumeric, the length
     being determined by the supplier.

General rules

1. Suppose that a parameter is followed by an indicator parameter. When the indicator parameter has a negative value then the value of the parameter specification equals the NULL value, and otherwise it equals the value of the parameter itself.

   In the following example the PAR1 parameter is set to the value of the maximum amount in the PENALTIES table and the IND1 parameter to zero. If, however, the PENALTIES table is empty or if the AMOUNT column only contains NULL values (which in our example is not possible), then the IND1 parameter is set to a negative value.

   ```
   SELECT   MAX(AMOUNT), MIN(AMOUNT)
   INTO     PAR1 INDICATOR IND1, PAR2 INDICATOR IND2
   FROM     PENALTIES
   ```

2. Suppose that a variable is followed by an indicator variable. When the indicator variable has a negative value the value of the variable specification equals the NULL value, and otherwise equals the value of the variable.

3. The value of the system variable USER is the same as the name of the user specified in the module.

Chapter 4

Definitions of the SQL statements

In this chapter we describe all the SQL statements included in the ISO standard. They are:

- CLOSE
- COMMIT
- CREATE SCHEMA
- CREATE TABLE
- CREATE VIEW
- DECLARE CURSOR
- DELETE
- FETCH
- GRANT
- INSERT
- MODULE
- OPEN
- PROCEDURE
- ROLLBACK
- SELECT
- UPDATE

For each statement we give:

- a description (what the statement does)
- the format; sometimes we also repeat definitions of the common elements in order to clarify the statements
- additional rules which are not included in the BNF, but are concerned with the syntax of SQL
- general rules which have to do with the meaning of statements
- examples

We present the statements in alphabetical order.

4.1 CLOSE

Description

The CLOSE statement is used to close a cursor which has been previously opened with an OPEN statement. From this point the cursor can only be used if it is reopened.

Format

```
<close statement> ::=
   CLOSE <cursor name>
```

Additional rules

1. The cursor must have been opened with an OPEN statement.

2. The module in which the cursor is closed ought to contain the definition of the cursor as well (DECLARE statement)

General rules

1. The cursor ought to have been previously opened.

2. The cursor is closed and is no longer accessible until it is reopened.

Examples

See DECLARE CURSOR.

4.2 COMMIT

Description

A COMMIT statement is used to terminate a successfully executed transaction.

Explanation: We define a *transaction* as a series of SQL operations on a database, which together form a unit with respect to *recovery* and *concurrency*. At the beginning of a program there are no active transactions. The first SQL statement in a program marks the beginning of a transaction. Each SQL statement executed afterwards belongs to the active transaction. A successfully executed transaction is terminated with a COMMIT statement and rolled back with a ROLLBACK statement. The moment at which a transaction is terminated or rolled back is sometimes called a *commit point*. The next SQL statement after a COMMIT or ROLLBACK begins the following transaction.

The SQL standard makes the following point about concurrent execution of transactions:

> *The execution of concurrent transactions is guaranteed to be serializable. A serializable execution is defined to be an execution of the operations of concurrently executing transactions that produces the same effect as some serial execution of those same transactions. A serial execution is one in which each transaction executes to completion before the next transaction begins.*

Format

```
<commit statement> ::=
   COMMIT WORK
```

General rules

1. The transaction ends, and all updates to the database become permanent.

2. All cursors which remain open are closed.

Examples

The example below shows part of a program. We have used Pascal as the host language. We have also omitted details in order to simplify the example.

```
    :
EXEC SQL
    UPDATE    PLAYERS
    SET       TOWN = 'Inglewood'
    WHERE     PLAYERNO = 27;
    :
IF <search condition> THEN
    EXEC SQL COMMIT WORK;
ELSE
    EXEC SQL ROLLBACK WORK;
    :
```

4.3 CREATE SCHEMA

Description

In the SQL standard each table and view belongs to a schema. At the same time as the schema is created so too are all the tables, views and privileges set up. The name of the user is also specified at this point. This user is the sole owner of the schema and all the tables and views which belong to it. Each user has a maximum of one schema. An entire database can contain many schemas.

Format

```
<schema> ::=
   CREATE SCHEMA AUTHORIZATION <authorization identifier>
   [ <schema element>... ]

<schema element> ::=
   <table definition> |
   <view definition> |
   <privilege definition>
```

Additional rules

1. Two schemas may not have the same authorization identifier. In other words, each user can own only one schema.

Examples

Create the schema for (a part of) the sample database and specify WILLIAM as the owner.

```
CREATE SCHEMA AUTHORIZATION WILLIAM

CREATE TABLE GAMES
      ( TEAMNO     SMALLINT     NOT NULL,
        PLAYERNO   SMALLINT     NOT NULL,
        WON        SMALLINT     NOT NULL,
        LOST       SMALLINT     NOT NULL,
        UNIQUE     (TEAMNO, PLAYERNO))


CREATE    VIEW PLAYERS_PER_TEAM (TEAMNO, NUMBER) AS
SELECT    TEAMNO, COUNT(*)
FROM      GAMES
GROUP BY  TEAMNO


GRANT     SELECT
ON        PLAYERS_PER_TEAM
TO        PUBLIC
```

4.4   CREATE TABLE

Description

A table is the only object in SQL where data can be stored. The CREATE
TABLE statement (or <table definition>) is used to create a so-called *base
table* with a set of integrity rules.

Format

```
<table definition> ::=
   CREATE TABLE <table name>
   ( <table element> [ {,<table element>}... ] )

<table name> ::=
   [ <authorization identifier>. ] <table identifier>

<table element> ::=
   <column definition> |
   <unique constraint definition>

<column definition> ::=
   <column name> <data type> [ NOT NULL [ UNIQUE ] ]

<unique constraint definition> ::=
   UNIQUE <column list>

<column list> ::=
   ( <column name> [ {,<column name>}... ] )

<data type> ::=
   CHARACTER [ ( <length> ) ] |
   CHAR      [ ( <length> ) ] |
   NUMERIC   [ ( <precision> [,<scale>] ) ] |
   DECIMAL   [ ( <precision> [,<scale>] ) ] |
   DEC       [ ( <precision> [,<scale>] ) ] |
   INTEGER   |
   INT       |
   SMALLINT  |
   FLOAT     [ ( <precision> ) ] |
   REAL      |
   DOUBLE PRECISION
```

Additional rules

1. If the name of a user precedes the table identifier then it must be the owner of the schema to which the table belongs. In a schema, therefore, no tables may be created for another owner.

2. No two tables or views in a schema may have the same name.

3. No two columns in a table may have the same name.

4. Each column specified as UNIQUE must also be specified as NOT NULL.

General rules

1. NOT NULL is an integrity rule. With this rule we determine that a particular column cannot contain NULL values.

2. UNIQUE is an integrity rule. It is used to specify that the same two values cannot occur in a particular column or combination of columns.

3. The integrity rules NOT NULL and UNIQUE are tested directly after the execution of each (relevant) SQL statement. If an UPDATE or INSERT statement (intentionally or unintentionally) violates one of the integrity rules SQL does not accept the statement and returns a negative value to the SQLCODE variable.

Examples

Create the PLAYERS table:

```
CREATE TABLE PLAYERS
       ( PLAYERNO       SMALLINT NOT NULL UNIQUE,
         NAME           CHAR(15) NOT NULL,
         INITIALS       CHAR(3)  NOT NULL,
         YEAR_OF_BIRTH  SMALLINT ,
         SEX            CHAR     NOT NULL,
         YEAR_JOINED    SMALLINT NOT NULL,
         STREET         CHAR(15) NOT NULL,
         HOUSENO        CHAR(4)  ,
         POSTCODE       CHAR(6)  ,
         TOWN           CHAR(10) NOT NULL,
         LEAGUENO       CHAR(4)  ,
         UNIQUE         (NAME, INITIALS))
```

We can also write this statement as follows (note the unique constraint definition on the PLAYERNO column):

```
CREATE TABLE PLAYERS
    ( PLAYERNO   SMALLINT    NOT NULL,
      NAME       CHAR(15)    NOT NULL,
      :
      :
      LEAGUENO   CHAR(4),
      UNIQUE     (PLAYERNO),
      UNIQUE     (NAME, INITIALS))
```

Create the GAMES table:

```
CREATE TABLE GAMES
    ( TEAMNO     SMALLINT    NOT NULL,
      PLAYERNO   SMALLINT    NOT NULL,
      WON        SMALLINT    NOT NULL,
      LOST       SMALLINT    NOT NULL,
      UNIQUE     (TEAMNO, PLAYERNO))
```

Because all the columns in the GAMES table have been defined as NOT NULL the following UPDATE statement would not be accepted even though it is syntactically correct.

```
UPDATE    GAMES
SET       LOST = NULL
WHERE     PLAYERNO = 27
```

4.5 CREATE VIEW

Description

A view is a table whose virtual contents are derived from one or more other tables or views. A SELECT statement is used to define the contents. A view, therefore, is also a table; a so-called *virtual table*.

Format

```
<view definition> ::=
    CREATE VIEW <table name>
        [ <column list> ]
        AS <query specification>
        [ WITH CHECK OPTION ]

<table name> ::=
    [ <authorization identifier>. ] <table identifier>

<column list> ::=
    ( <column name> [ {,<column name> }... ] )

<query specification> ::=
    SELECT [ ALL | DISTINCT ] <select list>
    <table expression>

<select list> ::=
    <value expression> [ {,<value expression>}... ] | *

<table expression> ::=
    <from clause>
    [ <where clause> ]
    [ <group by clause> ]
    [ <having clause> ]
```

Additional rules

1. If the name of a user precedes the name of the view, then that must be the owner of the schema to which the view belongs. Therefore, no views may be created in a schema for another owner.

2. The name of a view (table identifier) may not be the same as the name of a view or another table in that schema.

3. A view is updatable when the query specification from which it is built is updatable.

4. Two column names in the column list of a view may not be the same.

5. The number of column names in the column list must equal the number of value expressions in the select list.

6. When two columns in a query specification have the same name or when one of these columns has no name, a column list is mandatory. A column in a query specification has no name, for example, if it is the result of a calculation or the result of a set function specification.
   The use of a column list is mandatory in the next two examples.

```
CREATE     VIEW S1900
           (SNR, YEAR_TALLY) AS
SELECT     PLAYERNO, YEAR_OF_BIRTH - 1900
FROM       PLAYERS

CREATE     VIEW INHABITANTS
           (TOWN, NUMBER) AS
SELECT     TOWN, COUNT(*)
FROM       PLAYERS
GROUP BY TOWN
```

7. WITH CHECK OPTION may only be specified in cases where the view is updatable.

General rules

1. If a view 'WITH CHECK OPTION' is defined, all updates resulting from UPDATE and INSERT statements are tested:
   - An UPDATE statement is correct when the updated rows still form part of the (virtual) contents of the view after the update.
   - An INSERT statement is correct when the new rows belong to the (virtual) contents of the view.

Suppose we create this view:

```
CREATE     VIEW OLDIES AS
SELECT     *
FROM       PLAYERS
WHERE      YEAR_OF_BIRTH < 1950
WITH       CHECK OPTION
```

This view cannot be updated with the following UPDATE statement. The row which would be updated would no longer exist in the view.

```
UPDATE    OLDIES
SET       YEAR_OF_BIRTH = 1960
WHERE     PLAYERNO = 95
```

Examples

Create a view to show the numbers, the names, the initials and the year of birth of players who were born in Stratford.

```
CREATE    VIEW SFDPEOPLE AS
SELECT    PLAYERNO, NAME, INITIALS, YEAR_OF_BIRTH
FROM      PLAYERS
WHERE     TOWN = 'Stratford'
```

Create a view to show the numbers of the players who are younger than the player whose number is 6.

```
CREATE    VIEW YOUTH AS
SELECT    B.PLAYERNO
FROM      PLAYERS A, PLAYERS B
WHERE     A.YEAR_OF_BIRTH > B.YEAR_OF_BIRTH
AND       A.PLAYERNO = 6
```

4.6 DECLARE CURSOR

Description

A DECLARE statement is used to declare a so-called *cursor*. A cursor is a declaration of a query expression. The value of a cursor equals that of the result of the query expression. Cursors make it possible to return to a program, row by row, the result of a query expression, which could have an unlimited but finite number of rows.

Format

```
<declare cursor> ::=
   DECLARE <cursor name> CURSOR FOR
   <query expression>
   [ <order by clause> ]

<order by clause> ::=
   ORDER BY <sort specification>
            [ {,<sort specification>}... ]

<sort specification> ::=
   { <sequence number> | <column specification> }
   [ ASC | DESC ]

<sequence number> ::= <unsigned integer>
```

Additional rules

1. Two cursors may not have the same name within a module.

2. Each parameter used in the cursor ought to be declared.

3. Each sequence number in a sort specification must be greater than zero and less than or equal to the number of value expressions in the select list(s).

4. All column specifications which appear in a sort specification ought to be specified in the select list.

5. When UNION is used the select lists of the query specification must consist of '*' or of column specifications.

6. The result of a cursor declaration is only updatable if

- the query expression consists of a single query specification and therefore contains no UNION
- the query specification is updatable, and
- ORDER BY has *not* been used.

General rules

1. If ORDER BY is not specified, the sequence of the rows is supplier dependent.

2. When neither ASC nor DESC is specified the rows are sorted in ascending order.

Examples

Below we give an example of declaring a cursor and processing the result. The result of the CAPTAINS cursor contains the numbers and names of all captains. After the DECLARE statement the cursor is opened and the result determined. As long as the value of the SQLCODE variable is zero the result continues to be returned row by row with FETCH statements.

We have used Pascal as our host language. We have also omitted details in order to simplify the example.

```
    :
    EXEC SQL
        DECLARE   CAPTAINS CURSOR FOR
        SELECT    PLAYERNO, NAME
        FROM      PLAYERS
        WHERE     PLAYERNO IN
                  (SELECT   PLAYERNO
                   FROM     TEAMS);
    :
    EXEC SQL OPEN CAPTAINS;
    EXEC SQL FETCH CAPTAINS INTO PNO, NAME;
    WHILE SQLCODE = 0 DO
        BEGIN
           :
           EXEC SQL FETCH CAPTAINS INTO PNO, NAME;
        END;
    EXEC SQL CLOSE CAPTAINS;
    :
```

Three other examples:

```
DECLARE    SFDPEOPLE CURSOR FOR
SELECT     PLAYERNO, TOWN
FROM       PLAYERS
WHERE      TOWN = 'Stratford'
ORDER BY 1


DECLARE    TALLY CURSOR FOR
SELECT     WON
FROM       GAMES
UNION      ALL
SELECT     LOST
FROM       GAMES
ORDER BY 1 DESC


DECLARE    NAMES CURSOR FOR
SELECT     NAME, INITIALS, TOWN
FROM       PLAYERS
ORDER BY 1 DESC, INITIALS ASC, TOWN DESC
```

4.7 DELETE

Description

The DELETE statement is used to delete particular rows from a table.

Format

```
<delete statement> ::=
   DELETE FROM <table name>
   [ WHERE { CURRENT OF <cursor name> | <search condition> } ]

<table name> ::=
   [ <authorization identifier>. ] <table identifier>
```

Additional rules

1. The DELETE privilege for a table is necessary before a user can delete rows.

2. If no WHERE clause is specified all rows are deleted from the table.

3. When the WHERE clause identifies a cursor the following conditions apply:

    *   The module in which the DELETE statement sits ought to contain the definition of the cursor (DECLARE statement).

    *   The cursor must already have been opened with an OPEN statement and there must have been at least one FETCH statement performed on the cursor.

    *   The cursor must be updatable.

    *   The table name in the DELETE statement must be the same as the table name in the first FROM clause of the cursor's query specification.

Examples

Delete all penalties incurred by player 44.

```
DELETE
FROM      PENALTIES
WHERE     PLAYERNO = 44
```

Delete all competition data about players who live in Stratford.

```
DELETE
FROM      GAMES
WHERE     PLAYERNO IN
          (SELECT   PLAYERNO
           FROM     PLAYERS
           WHERE    TOWN = 'Stratford')
```

Delete rows via a cursor. We use Pascal again as the host language. In order
to simplify the example we have omitted the details.

```
:
EXEC SQL
    DECLARE  C_PLAYERS CURSOR FOR
    SELECT   PLAYERNO, NAME
    FROM     PLAYERS
    WHERE    PLAYERNO = 'Stratford';
:
EXEC SQL OPEN C_PLAYERS;
EXEC SQL FETCH C_PLAYERS INTO PNO, NAME;
WHILE SQLCODE = 0 DO
    BEGIN
        IF <search condition> THEN
            EXEC SQL DELETE FROM PLAYERS
                     WHERE   CURRENT OF C_PLAYERS;
        :
        EXEC SQL FETCH C_PLAYERS INTO PNO, NAME;
    END;
EXEC SQL CLOSE C_PLAYERS;
:
```

4.8 FETCH

Description

A FETCH statement is used to retrieve the 'following' row in the result of a cursor. When the cursor has not yet been accessed with a FETCH statement the first row is retrieved.

Format

```
<fetch statement> ::=
   FETCH <cursor name>
   INTO <target specification>
       [ {,<target specification>}... ]

<target specification> ::=
   <parameter specification> |
   <variable specification>

<parameter specification> ::=
   <parameter name> [ [ INDICATOR ] <indicator parameter> ]

<variable specification> ::=
   <variable name> [ [ INDICATOR ] <indicator variable> ]
```

Additional rules

1. The module in which the FETCH statement sits ought to contain the definition of the cursor (DECLARE statement).

2. The number of target specifications must equal the number of value expressions in the select list in the cursor.

3. The data types of the target specifications and the value expressions in the select list of the cursor must be consistent.

General rules

1. The cursor must already have been opened with an OPEN statement.

2. When the result of a value expression in the select list of a cursor is a NULL value, the corresponding indicator parameter or variable is set to a negative value. In all other cases it is set to zero.

3. If the FETCH statement returns no rows the SQLCODE variable is set to 100.

Examples

See DECLARE CURSOR.

4.9 GRANT

Description

The GRANT statement (or <privilege definition>) is used to give users privileges. A privilege is always granted for a particular table. SQL recognizes the following privileges:

- SELECT: privilege to query a table
- INSERT: privilege to add new rows to a table
- UPDATE: privilege to change values in a table
- DELETE: privilege to remove rows from a table

Format

```
<privilege definition> ::=
   GRANT <privileges>
   ON    <table name>
   TO    <grantees>
   [ WITH GRANT OPTION ]

<privileges> ::=
   ALL PRIVILEGES |
   <action> [ {,<action>}... ]

<action> ::=
   SELECT |
   INSERT |
   DELETE |
   UPDATE <column list>

<column list> ::=
   ( [ <column name> [ {,<column name>}... ] ] )

<table name> ::=
   [ <authorization identifier>. ] <table identifier>

<grantees> ::=
   PUBLIC |
   <authorization identifier>
      [ {,<authorization identifier>}... ]
```

Additional rules

1. Each column name specified in the list of UPDATE privileges must be contained in the table for which the privilege is given.

2. ALL PRIVILEGES is equivalent to the sum of the privileges SELECT, INSERT, DELETE and UPDATE (for all columns).

3. When the column list is omitted with the UPDATE privilege, the implication is that the privilege applies to *all* columns in the table concerned.

4. The privileges INSERT, UPDATE and DELETE can only be granted for updatable tables.

5. An owner may grant the SELECT, INSERT, DELETE and UPDATE privileges for his or her own base table.

6. An owner of a view, if the view is *not* updatable, may only grant the SELECT privilege for this view when he or she has the SELECT privilege on all the tables and views named in the query specification of the view.

7. An owner of a view, if the view *is* updatable, may grant all the privileges he or she has on the table named in the query specification.

8. Each user who gets privileges with the WITH GRANT OPTION may pass these privileges on to other users.

Examples

Give JANE the SELECT privilege for the PLAYERS table.

```
GRANT     SELECT
ON        PLAYERS
TO        JANE
```

Give PETE the UPDATE privilege for the PLAYERNO and DIVISION columns of the TEAMS table:

```
GRANT     UPDATE (PLAYERNO, DIVISION)
ON        TEAMS
TO        PETE
```

Give JOHN the INSERT and UPDATE privileges (for all columns) for the
TEAMS table, which he can pass on to other users:

```
GRANT    INSERT, UPDATE
ON       TEAMS
TO       JOHN
WITH     GRANT OPTION
```

Give every user the SELECT privilege on the TEAMS table.

```
GRANT    SELECT
ON       TEAMS
TO       PUBLIC
```

4.10 INSERT

Description

The INSERT statement has two forms. With the first form one row of new values is inserted into a table. With the second form a set of rows is inserted into a table.

Format

```
<insert statement> ::=
   INSERT INTO <table name>
   [ <column list> ]
   { VALUES ( <value> {,<value>}... ) | <query specification> }

<table name> ::=
   [ <authorization identifier>. ] <table identifier>

<column list> ::=
   ( <column name> [ {,<column name> }... ] )

<value> ::=
   <value specification> | NULL

<query specification> ::=
   SELECT [ ALL | DISTINCT ] <select list>
   <table expression>

<select list> ::=
   <value expression> [ {,<value expression>}... ] | *

<table expression> ::=
   <from clause>
   [ <where clause> ]
   [ <group by clause> ]
   [ <having clause> ]
```

Additional rules

1. An INSERT statement may only be issued by a user who has the INSERT authority for the table concerned.

2. Any table into which rows are inserted must be updatable.

3. The number of columns in the column list must equal the number of values or the number of value expressions in the query specification.

4. The data types of the columns in the column list must be consistent with the data types of the value expressions in the select list.

General rules

1. The INSERT privilege on a table is necessary in order to be able to insert rows.

2. If, after the processing of the INSERT statement, it appears that no rows have been added (for example if the result of the query specification is empty), the SQLCODE variable is set to 100.

Examples

Insert a new team into the TEAMS table.

```
INSERT INTO TEAMS
        (TEAMNO, PLAYERNO, DIVISION)
VALUES (3, 100, 'third')
```

or:

```
INSERT INTO TEAMS (PLAYERNO, DIVISION, TEAMNO)
VALUES (100, 'third', 3)
```

We need an extra table for the next example.

```
CREATE TABLE RECREATION
        (PLAYERNO    SMALLINT NOT NULL UNIQUE,
         NAME        CHAR(15) NOT NULL,
         TOWN        CHAR(10) NOT NULL,
         PHONENO     CHAR(10)          )
```

The following INSERT populates the RECREATION table with data about recreational players registered in the PLAYERS table.

```
INSERT    INTO RECREATION
          (PLAYERNO, NAME, TOWN, PHONENO)
SELECT    PLAYERNO, NAME, TOWN, PHONENO
FROM      PLAYERS
WHERE     LEAGUENO IS NULL
```

4.11 MODULE

Description

MODULE is the statement used to create a set of procedures. A module is
linked to a program (for example, a FORTRAN program).

Format

```
<module> ::=
    MODULE         [ <module name> ]
    LANGUAGE       <programming language>
    AUTHORIZATION  <authorization identifier>
    [ <declare cursor>... ]
    <procedure>...

<programming language> ::=
    COBOL | FORTRAN | PASCAL | PLI

<declare cursor> ::=
    DECLARE <cursor name> CURSOR FOR
    <query expression>
    [ <order by clause> ]

<procedure> ::=
    PROCEDURE <procedure name> <parameter declaration>...;
    <sql statement>
```

Additional rules

1. Two modules may not have the same name.

2. For each cursor declaration in a module there must be at least one procedure in the module in which the cursor is opened.

3. A module must be linked to a program during execution. A program can
call only a single module.

4. The user/owner of a module must have sufficient privileges to execute all
the SQL statements in the module. If, for example, in one of the modules
a SELECT statement on the PLAYERS table is executed, then the user
must have the SELECT privilege on this table.

General rules

1. After a program has called a procedure in a module for the last time, a commit or rollback is automatically performed. (The choice of commit or rollback is left to the supplier.)

2. The way in which procedures are called from programs is not laid down in the standard and is, therefore, supplier dependent.

Examples

The following module contains only one procedure. Using a SELECT statement the procedure determines the year of birth of a player, given a particular player number.

```
MODULE EXAMPLE
    LANGUAGE PASCAL
    AUTHORIZATION WILLIAM

PROCEDURE FIND_YEAR_OF_BIRTH
    SQLCODE         INTEGER
    PNO             SMALLINT
    YEAR_OF_BIRTH   SMALLINT;
SELECT    PLAYERS.YEAR_OF_BIRTH
INTO      YEAR_OF_BIRTH
FROM      PLAYERS
WHERE     PLAYERS.PLAYERNO = PNO
```

As an example, we take the program from Section 4.6 (DECLARE CURSOR) and, instead of using embedded SQL, execute it here from a procedure. We have used Pascal as our host language and have omitted details in order to simplify the example. We assume that the special Pascal procedure, SQLCALL, takes care of the passing of parameters. We give the Pascal program first followed by the module.

```
PROGRAM EXAMPLE;
:
VAR PNO     : INTEGER;
    NAME    : PACKED ARRAY [1..10] OF CHAR;
    SQLCODE : INTEGER;
:
BEGIN
:
SQLCALL ('OPEN_CAPTAINS');
SQLCALL ('FETCH_1_CAPTAIN');
WHILE SQLCODE = 0 DO
   BEGIN
      :
      SQLCALL ('FETCH_1_CAPTAIN');
   END;
SQLCALL ('CLOSE_CAPTAINS');
:
END;
```

The module:

```
MODULE ALL_CAPTAINS
   LANGUAGE PASCAL
   AUTHORIZATION RICK

DECLARE  CAPTAINS CURSOR FOR
SELECT   PLAYERNO, NAME
FROM     PLAYERS
WHERE    PLAYERNO IN
         (SELECT   PLAYERNO
          FROM     TEAMS)

PROCEDURE OPEN_CAPTAINS
   SQLCODE;
   OPEN CAPTAINS

PROCEDURE FETCH_1_CAPTAIN
   SQLCODE
   PNO     : INTEGER
   NAME    : CHARACTER(10);
   EXEC SQL FETCH CAPTAINS INTO PNO, NAME

PROCEDURE CLOSE_CAPTAINS
   SQLCODE;
   CLOSE CAPTAINS
```

4.12 OPEN

Description

An OPEN statement is used to open a cursor. By *open* we mean that the query expression specified in the declaration of the cursor has been executed. After the OPEN and FETCH statements are issued the result of the query expression is returned row by row.

Format

```
<open statement> ::=
   OPEN <cursor name>
```

Additional rules

1.   The module in which the cursor is opened ought to contain the definition of the cursor (DECLARE statement).

General rules

1.   The cursor may not already be open when the OPEN statement is issued.

2.   The first FETCH statement returns the first row of the result of the query expression.

Examples

See DECLARE CURSOR.

4.13 PROCEDURE

Description

A procedure is embedded in a module and contains one DML statement. A procedure can be called from a program written in another programming language.

Format

```
<procedure> ::=
   PROCEDURE <procedure name> <parameter declaration>...;
   <sql statement>

<parameter declaration> ::=
   <parameter name> <data type> | SQLCODE

<sql statement> ::=
   <close statement>   |
   <commit statement>  |
   <delete statement>  |
   <fetch statement>   |
   <insert statement>  |
   <open statement>    |
   <rollback statement> |
   <select statement>  |
   <update statement>

<data type> ::=
   CHARACTER [ ( <length> ) ] |
   CHAR      [ ( <length> ) ] |
   NUMERIC   [ ( <precision> [,<scale>] ) ] |
   DECIMAL   [ ( <precision> [,<scale>] ) ] |
   DEC       [ ( <precision> [,<scale>] ) ] |
   INTEGER   |
   INT       |
   SMALLINT  |
   FLOAT     [ ( <precision> ) ] |
   REAL      |
   DOUBLE PRECISION
```

Additional rules

1. Two procedures within a module may not have the same name.

2. Two parameters within a procedure may not have the same name.

3. Each parameter used in an SQL statement ought to be declared in the procedure.

4. If a column name in an SQL statement is the same as the name of a parameter named in the procedure where the SQL statement is defined, then a table name must precede the column name.

5. When the procedure is called from a program, you must pass as many values as there are declared parameters in the procedure.

6. The SQLCODE parameter may be declared only once in a procedure.

7. The SQLCODE parameter has a data type of INTEGER.

8. Each language differs in how parameters must be declared. The table below illustrates this. If a programming language does not support a particular data type, parameters of this type cannot be used.
   Note: 'pc' stands for a supplier dependent precision greater than or equal to 15. An 'x' stands for <nines>; see Chapter 5 for the definition of this.

SQL datatype	COBOL	FORTRAN	Pascal	PL/I
CHAR(n)	PIC X(n)	CHAR-ACTER*n	PACKED AR-RAY [1..n] OF CHAR	CHAR(n)
NUMERIC(p,s)	PIC SxVx DIS-PLAY SIGN LEADING SEPARATE	—	—	—
DECIMAL(p,s)	—	—	—	FIXED REAL DECI-MAL(p,s)
INTEGER	—	INTEGER	INTEGER	—
SMALLINT	—	—	—	—
FLOAT(p)	—	—	—	FLOAT REAL BINARY(p)
REAL	—	REAL	REAL	—
DOUBLE PRECISION	—	DOUBLE PRECISION	—	—
SQLCODE variable	Sx COMP	INTEGER	INTEGER	FIXED BINARY (pc)

Examples

Develop a procedure which determines the year of birth of a player, given a player number.

```
PROCEDURE FIND_YEAR_OF_BIRTH
    SQLCODE         INTEGER
    PLAYERNO        SMALLINT
    YEAR_OF_BIRTH   SMALLINT;
SELECT   PLAYERS.YEAR_OF_BIRTH
INTO     YEAR_OF_BIRTH
FROM     PLAYERS
WHERE    PLAYERS.PLAYERNO = PLAYERNO
```

See also MODULE.

4.14   ROLLBACK

Description

The ROLLBACK statement is used to undo all updates which have been performed during the active transaction, and terminates the transaction. See also the description of the COMMIT statement.

Format

```
<rollback statement> ::=
   ROLLBACK WORK
```

General rules

1.   All remaining open cursors are closed.

2.   All updates to the database are undone.

3.   The active transaction is terminated.

Examples

See COMMIT statement.

4.15 SELECT

Description

A SELECT statement is used to select one or no rows from a table.

Format

```
<select statement> ::=
    SELECT  [ ALL | DISTINCT ] <select list>
    INTO    <target specification>
            [ {,<target specification>}... ]
    <table expression>

<select list> ::=
    <value expression> [ {, <value expression> }... ] | *

<target specification> ::=
    <parameter specification> |
    <variable specification>

<parameter specification> ::=
    <parameter name> [ [ INDICATOR ] <indicator parameter> ]

<variable specification> ::=
    <variable name> [ [ INDICATOR ] <indicator variable> ]

<table expression> ::=
    <from clause>
    [ <where clause> ]
    [ <group by clause> ]
    [ <having clause> ]
```

Additional rules

1. A SELECT statement may only be issued if the user has the SELECT privilege on the table or tables concerned.

2. A table expression may *not* contain GROUP BY or HAVING clauses.

3. The FROM clause in the table expression may not contain a grouped view.

4. The number of elements in the select expression must equal the number of target specifications.

5. The data types of the target specifications and the value expressions in the select list must be consistent.

General rules

1. The result of a SELECT statement must consist of one or zero rows.

2. If a SELECT statement returns no rows, the SQLCODE is set to the value 100; otherwise it is set to zero.

3. DISTINCT is used to group duplicate rows. DISTINCT recognizes two NULL values as equal to one another, this being the opposite to all the comparison operators.

Examples

Give the year of birth and the town of player 27.

```
SELECT    YEAR_OF_BIRTH, TOWN
INTO      YOB INDICATOR IND1, TWN
FROM      PLAYERS
WHERE     PLAYERNO = 27
```

Give the number of players.

```
SELECT    COUNT(*)
INTO      NUMBER
FROM      PLAYERS
```

4.16   UPDATE

Description

The UPDATE statement is used to alter the values of existing rows in a table.

Format

```
<update statement> ::=
   UPDATE <table name>
   SET    <object column> [ {,<object column>}... ]
   [ WHERE { CURRENT OF <cursor name> |
             <search condition> } ]

<table name> ::=
   [ <authorization identifier>. ] <table identifier>

<object column> ::=
   <column name> = { <value expression> | NULL }
```

Additional rules

1. The UPDATE privilege on a table is necessary before the user can alter the contents.

2. If there is no WHERE clause specified, all rows are updated.

3. If the update NULL is specified the column cannot have been defined as NOT NULL.

4. The value expression in the update may *not* contain a set function specification.

5. If a cursor is referenced in the WHERE clause then the following conditions hold:

    *   The module in which the UPDATE statement sits ought to contain the definition of the cursor (DECLARE statement).

    *   The cursor must already have been opened with an OPEN statement.

    *   The cursor must be updatable.

    *   The table name in the UPDATE statement must be the same as the table name in the first FROM clause of the cursor's query specification.

General rules

1. If the UPDATE statement updates no rows, the SQLCODE variable is set to the value 100.

Examples

Update the league number of player 95 to 2000.

```
UPDATE PLAYERS
SET    LEAGUENO = '2000'
WHERE  PLAYERNO = 95
```

Increase all penalties by 5 per cent.

```
UPDATE   PENALTIES
SET      AMOUNT = AMOUNT * 1.05
```

The Parmenter family shifts house to 83 Plane Street in Inglewood, the post-code becomes 1234 UU, telephone number unknown.

```
UPDATE   PLAYERS
SET      STREET   = 'Plane Street',
         HOUSENO  = '83',
         TOWN     = 'Inglewood',
         POSTCODE = '1234UU',
         PHONENO  = NULL
WHERE    NAME     = 'Parmenter'
```

Update rows in a table using a cursor. We have used Pascal as the host language. We have omitted details in order to simplify the example.

```
    :
EXEC SQL
    DECLARE   C_PLAYERS CURSOR FOR
    SELECT    PLAYERNO, NAME
    FROM      PLAYERS
    WHERE     PLAYERNO = 'Stratford';
    :
EXEC SQL OPEN C_PLAYERS;
EXEC SQL FETCH C_PLAYERS INTO PNO, NAME;
WHILE SQLCODE = 0 DO
    BEGIN
        :
        IF <search condition> THEN
            EXEC SQL
                UPDATE   PLAYERS
                SET      YEAR_OF_BIRTH = 1975
                WHERE    CURRENT OF C_PLAYERS;
        :
        EXEC SQL FETCH C_PLAYERS INTO PNO, NAME;
    END;
EXEC SQL CLOSE C_PLAYERS;
    :
```

Chapter 5

Embedded SQL

The SQL standard has a number of annexes which describe the so-called *embedded SQL*. By embedded SQL we mean that SQL statements are included in a program written in another programming language, such as COBOL or FORTRAN. In this environment we call such a language a *host language*.

These annexes about embedded SQL do *not* form part of the standard. Therefore, a supplier does not have to support embedded SQL in order to conform with the standard.

Embedded SQL has been described in the annexes for the following languages (we also give the ISO publication numbers of the standards document for each of the languages):

- COBOL (ISO 1539)
- FORTRAN (ISO 1989)
- Pascal (ISO 6160)
- PL/I (ISO 7185)

Before we begin to include SQL statements in a program we need to consider the following points:

- how do we show that a particular statement belongs to SQL and not to the host language?

- how do we declare the variables to be used in SQL statements?

- how should a program react to the value of the SQLCODE variable after having executed an SQL statement?

5.1 Indicating SQL statements

A program with embedded SQL consists of host language statements interspersed with SQL statements. To differentiate SQL statements from other statements, in whatever language, they must all be preceded by the following prefix:

    EXEC SQL

Each statement must also be terminated with a special delimiter. Each programming language has its own way of terminating an SQL statement. In COBOL it is:

    END-EXEC

In Pascal and PL/I the SQL statements end in a semi-colon (;). FORTRAN does not recognize any end-of-statement delimiters. Instead, a statement is terminated if there is no continuation character in the sixth position of the following record.

All SQL statements, apart from DECLARE SECTION and WHENEVER, can be put anywhere in a program where an executable statement is permitted. For COBOL, for example, this is the PROCEDURE DIVISION.

5.2 Declaring variables

Host language variables which are used in an SQL statement (for example in a SELECT statement), must be declared in a special section in the program. We mark the beginning of this section with:

    BEGIN DECLARE SECTION

And at the end we write:

    END DECLARE SECTION

Of course these statements must be preceded by the prefix described above and terminated appropriately depending on the host language. In this section it is mandatory to declare at least the SQLCODE (SQLCOD in a FORTRAN program).

The declaration of variables looks different for each of above-mentioned host languages. Below we give the syntax for each of the four languages.

```
<cobol variable definition> ::=
   { 01 | 77 } <cobol variable> <cobol data type>

<cobol data type> ::=
   { PIC | PICTURE } [ IS ] X ( <unsigned integer> ) |
   { PIC | PICTURE } [ IS ] S <nines> [ V <nines> ]
      [ USAGE [ IS ] ] DISPLAY SIGN LEADING SEPARATE |
   { PIC | PICTURE } [ IS ] S <nines> V
      [ USAGE [ IS ] ] DISPLAY SIGN LEADING SEPARATE |
   { PIC | PICTURE } [ IS ] S V <nines>
      [ USAGE [ IS ] ] DISPLAY SIGN LEADING SEPARATE |
   { PIC | PICTURE } [ IS ] S <nines>
      [ USAGE [ IS ] ] { COMPUTATIONAL | COMP }

<nines> ::= { 9 [<unsigned integer>] }...

<fortran variable definition> ::=
   CHARACTER [ *<length> ] <fortran variable> |
   INTEGER <fortran variable> |
   REAL <fortran variable> |
   DOUBLE PRECISION <fortran variable>

<pascal variable definition> ::=
   <pascal variable> :
      PACKED ARRAY [ 1..<length> ] OF CHAR |
   <pascal variable> : INTEGER |
   <pascal variable> : REAL

<pl1 variable definition> ::=
   { DCL | DECLARE }
   { <pl1 variable> |
     ( <pl1 variable> [ {,<pl1 variable>}... ] ) }
   <pl1 data type>

<pl1 data type> ::=
   { CHARACTER | CHAR } ( <length> )           |
   DECIMAL FIXED ( <precision> [ ,<scale> ] ) |
   FIXED DECIMAL ( <precision> [ ,<scale> ] ) |
   BINARY FIXED  [ ( <precision> ) ]          |
   FIXED BINARY  [ ( <precision> ) ]          |
   BINARY FLOAT  ( <precision> )              |
   FLOAT BINARY  ( <precision> )
```

The data type which we assign to a variable depends on how it will be used in an SQL statement. In the table below we show, for each of the four programming languages, how the variable must be declared for a given SQL data type.

Note: In the column for COBOL we have placed an 'x' for <nines>; see the COBOL data types above.

SQL data type	COBOL	FORTRAN	Pascal	PL/I
CHAR(n)	PIC X(n)	CHAR-ACTER*n	PACKED AR-RAY [1..n] OF CHAR	CHAR(n)
NUMERIC(p,s)	PIC SxVx DIS-PLAY SIGN LEADING SEPARATE	—	—	—
DECIMAL(p,s)	—	—	—	FIXED DECI-MAL(p,s)
INTEGER	PIC Sx COMP	INTEGER	INTEGER	FIXED BINARY
SMALLINT	—	—	—	—
FLOAT(p)	—	—	—	FLOAT BINARY(p)
REAL	—	REAL	REAL	—
DOUBLE PRECISION	—	DOUBLE PRECISION	—	—

5.3 WHENEVER

Description

One statement has been added to SQL so that it can be embedded in a program. The WHENEVER statement (referred to as the embedded exception declaration) can only be used in a host language program and therefore not in modules.

Format

```
<embedded exception condition> ::=
   WHENEVER <condition> <exception action>

<condition> ::=
   SQLERROR | NOT FOUND

<exception action> ::=
   CONTINUE        |
   GOTO <target> |
   GO TO <target>
```

Additional rules

1. The target to which the program must 'jump' has to conform to the syntax of the host language. In COBOL, for example, it should be a valid section name and in FORTRAN a positive integer.

2. The WHENEVER statement applies to all SQL statements which follow it, until the end of the program is reached or until the next WHENEVER statement occurs.

Explanation

In principle, the SQLCODE should test the return code of every executed SQL statement. The value of this special variable identifies what has happened. There are four possible situations:

- value is negative: an error has occurred
- value is zero: everything has executed correctly
- value is one hundred: no rows have been returned
- value is greater than zero: a warning has been issued

A *precompiler* processes WHENEVER statements. The precompiler places a number of IF statements after each SQL statement; one for each condition. The generated IF statements consist of a condition, in which the SQLCODE is tested, and an action. If the action of a condition is to CONTINUE, then the precompiler generates *no* IF statements. Otherwise, the precompiler generates a GOTO statement which is consistent with the action specified in the WHENEVER statement. The return code 'SQLCODE < 0' is generated for the condition SQLERROR, whereas 'SQLCODE = 100' is generated for the condition NOT FOUND.

5.4 Example of a program with embedded SQL

Below we present a FORTRAN program which contains embedded SQL. The program prints all the team numbers which occur in the TEAMS table.

```
          PROGRAM ALL
C
C         VARIABLES
C         ------------------------------------------------
          EXEC SQL BEGIN DECLARE SECTION
          INTEGER  SQLCOD
          INTEGER  TEAMNO
          EXEC SQL END DECLARE SECTION
C
C         ERROR HANDLING
C         ------------------------------------------------
          EXEC SQL WHENEVER SQLERROR  GOTO 900
          EXEC SQL WHENEVER NOT FOUND CONTINUE
C
C         CURSOR DECLARATION
C         ------------------------------------------------
          EXEC SQL DECLARE TEAMS CURSOR FOR
        1      SELECT   TEAMNO
        2      FROM     TEAMS
C
C         PRINT ALL TEAM NUMBERS
C         ------------------------------------------------
          PRINT *, 'TEAMS'
          PRINT *, '-----'
          EXEC SQL OPEN TEAMS
  100     EXEC SQL FETCH TEAMS INTO TEAMNO
          IF (SQLCOD .NE. 0) GO TO 200
              PRINT *, TEAMNO
          GO TO 100
  200     EXEC SQL CLOSE TEAMS
  900     END
```

The same program in Pascal looks like this:

```
PROGRAM ALL;

EXEC SQL BEGIN DECLARE SECTION;
   SQLCODE : INTEGER;
   TEAMNO  : INTEGER;
EXEC SQL END DECLARE SECTION;

EXEC SQL WHENEVER SQLERROR  GOTO 900;
EXEC SQL WHENEVER NOT FOUND CONTINUE;

EXEC SQL DECLARE TEAMS CURSOR FOR
   SELECT   TEAMNO
   FROM     TEAMS;

BEGIN
   WRITELN('TEAMS');
   WRITELN('-----');
   EXEC SQL OPEN TEAMS;
   EXEC SQL FETCH TEAMS INTO TEAMNO;
   WHILE SQLCODE = 0 DO
      BEGIN
         WRITELN(TEAMNO);
         EXEC SQL FETCH TEAMS INTO TEAMNO;
      END;
   EXEC SQL CLOSE TEAMS;

900:

END.
```

Chapter 6

The two levels of the SQL standard

Two *levels* of the SQL standard have been defined. Level 2 contains all the SQL statements and definitions which we discussed in Chapters 3 and 4. Level 1 is a subset of level 2. In fact, level 2 encompasses level 1. The following definitions do not occur in level 1:

- The length of identifiers for objects such as tables and views is restricted to twelve positions.

- In the definition of a table name it is not possible to give an authorization identifier.

- The system variable USER, the indicator parameter and the indicator variable disappear from the definition of a value specification.

- The word 'ALL' is missing from the set function specification. In level 1 it is automatically assumed that if the word 'DISTINCT' is left out, duplicate rows may not be deleted.

- AVG, MAX, MIN and SUM may not be used with the distinct set function; only the COUNT set function is permitted.

- The comparison operator <> disappears. To formulate the search condition 'a <> b' one writes 'NOT (a = b)'.

- The escape character is not available with the LIKE operator.

- As well, with the LIKE operator, 'a NOT LIKE b' is not supported. This search condition is rewritten as 'NOT (a LIKE b)'.

- EXISTS as a predicate is removed.

- The way in which NULL values are grouped is left up to the supplier to decide.

- There are no schemas.

- It is not possible to specify a unique constraint definition or UNIQUE in the CREATE TABLE statement.

- The data types REAL, DOUBLE PRECISION and NUMERIC disappear.

- NOT NULL *must* be specified in every column definition in a CREATE TABLE statement.

- The WITH CHECK OPTION in the CREATE VIEW statement is omitted.

- The WITH GRANT OPTION in the GRANT statement disappears.

- The only parameters which may be passed in a procedure are those with a data type of CHARACTER.

- In the SQL standard the SQLCODE 100 means that no rows have been found. In level 1 the SQLCODE variable for the equivalent situation is decided upon by the supplier.

- It is not possible to use sequence numbers to indicate sorting in the ORDER BY clause.

- The possibility of specifying ASC in the ORDER BY clause disappears. The omission of the word 'DESC' automatically implies ascending order.

- It is not possible to combine results of SELECT statements with UNION.

- There is no facility for placing query specifications in INSERT statements.

- The search condition 'CURRENT OF ...' disappears from the DELETE and UPDATE statements.

- The definition of a transaction becomes: 'A transaction is a sequence of operations, including database operations, that is atomic with respect to recovery.'

Chapter 7

Addendum 1: Integrity enhancements

After the completion of the SQL standard the authors developed an addendum; see [ISO87b]. This addendum contains a number of new possibilities for defining integrity rules or constraint definitions. No new SQL statements have been introduced in the addendum; rather, the table and privilege definitions have been extended. In this chapter we discuss the adapted definitions and rules. In Appendix A (in this book) we list the reserved words which have been added.

Note: The integrity enhancements which we are discussing will also be included in the SQL standard.

7.1   CREATE TABLE

Description

A table is the only object in SQL in which data can be stored. The CREATE
TABLE statement is used to create a so-called *base table* with a set of integrity
rules (or constraint definitions).

Format

```
<table definition> ::=
   CREATE TABLE <table name>
   ( <table element> [ {,<table element>}... ] )

<table element> ::=
   <column definition> |
   <table constraint definition>

<column definition> ::=
   <column name> <data type>
   [ DEFAULT { <literal> | USER | NULL } ]
   [ <column constraint definition>... ]

<column constraint definition> ::=
   NOT NULL [ UNIQUE | PRIMARY KEY ] |
   <foreign key> |
   <check constraint definition>

<table constraint definition> ::=
   <unique constraint definition> |
   <referential constraint definition> |
   <check constraint definition>

<unique constraint definition> ::=
   { UNIQUE | PRIMARY KEY } <column list>

<referential constraint definition> ::=
   FOREIGN KEY <column list>
   <foreign key>

<foreign key> ::=
   REFERENCES <table name> [ <column list> ]
```

```
<check constraint definition> ::=
   CHECK ( <search condition> )

<table name> ::=
   [ <authorization identifier>. ] <table identifier>

<column list> ::=
   ( <column name> [ {,<column name>}... ] )

<data type> ::=
   CHARACTER [ ( <length> ) ] |
   CHAR      [ ( <length> ) ] |
   NUMERIC   [ ( <precision> [,<scale>]) ] ] |
   DECIMAL   [ ( <precision> [,<scale>]) ] ] |
   DEC       [ ( <precision> [,<scale>]) ] ] |
   INTEGER   |
   INT       |
   SMALLINT  |
   FLOAT     [ ( <precision> ) ] |
   REAL      |
   DOUBLE PRECISION
```

Additional rules

1. If the name of a user is specified before a table identifier, it must be the owner of the schema to which the table belongs. In a schema, therefore, no tables can be created for another user.

2. No two tables or views in the same schema may have the same name.

3. No two columns in the same table may have the same name.

4. NOT NULL *may* be specified after the data type of a column. The use of NOT NULL prevents NULL values from being stored in the column concerned.

5. The specification PRIMARY KEY may be used only once in a CREATE TABLE statement.

6. The specifications UNIQUE or PRIMARY KEY after a column name mean that the column concerned may not contain duplicate values.

7. Each column defined as UNIQUE or PRIMARY KEY must also be defined as NOT NULL.

8. If NOT NULL is not specified for column C, then the implication is: 'C DEFAULT NULL.' If NOT NULL *is* specified then it is a shortened notation for CHECK (<column name> IS NOT NULL).

9. When a check constraint definition (CHECK) is included straight after the column definition, then each column specification used in the search condition must refer to the column on which the constraint definition is defined. In the constraint definition for the column definition below *only* the YEAR_OF_BIRTH column can be named:

    ```
    YEAR_OF_BIRTH INTEGER CHECK(YEAR_OF_BIRTH < 1988)
    ```

    If, however, the check constraint definition is defined separately, then the search condition can contain only column specifications which refer to columns defined in the table. In this next constraint definition, therefore, all columns from the PLAYERS table may be used:

    ```
    CREATE    TABLE PLAYERS
              (PLAYERNO    SMALLINT
                           NOT NULL
                           PRIMARY KEY,
              :
              :
              LEAGUENO    CHAR(4),
              UNIQUE      (NAME, INITIALS),
              CHECK       (YEAR_OF_BIRTH < YEAR_JOINED))
    ```

10. A check constraint definition may *not* contain subqueries. The construction below, then, is *incorrect*:

    ```
    CHECK (PLAYERNO IN (SELECT PLAYERNO FROM PENALTIES))
    ```

11. If the DEFAULT value of a column is USER, then this column must be given a data type of CHARACTER.

12. If the DEFAULT value of a column is NULL, then the column may not be defined as NOT NULL.

13. The table named in a referential constraint definition must be a base table. It must have been created from a TABLE definition.

14. The number of columns in the two column lists of a referential constraint definition must be equal.

15. A column may not appear twice in one of the column lists of a referential constraint definition.

16. Each column referenced in a unique constraint definition must be defined as NOT NULL.

17. In cases where the second column list is omitted, the referenced table has a PRIMARY KEY.

General rules

1. NOT NULL is an integrity rule. By this we mean that a particular column may not contain NULL values.

2. The columns defined as PRIMARY KEY form the so-called primary key of the table.

3. UNIQUE and PRIMARY KEY are integrity rules. By this we mean that a particular column or combination of columns may not contain duplicate values.

4. The integrity rules NOT NULL, UNIQUE and PRIMARY KEY are tested immediately after the execution of each (relevant) SQL statement. If an (intentional or unintentional) UPDATE or INSERT statement breaches one of the integrity rules, SQL does not accept the statement and returns a negative value to the SQLCODE variable.

5. The referencing and referenced table satisfy the referential constraint definition when, for each row from the referencing table, one of these two conditions apply:

   - None of the referencing columns contains a NULL value and the referenced table contains at least one row in which there is a correspondence (of equal values) between each referencing column and each referenced column.

   - One of the referencing columns contains a NULL value.

Examples

Create the four tables in the sports club sample database.

```
CREATE    TABLE PLAYERS
          (PLAYERNO      SMALLINT
                         NOT NULL
                         PRIMARY KEY,
           NAME          CHAR(15)
                         NOT NULL,
           INITIALS      CHAR(3)
                         NOT NULL,
           YEAR_OF_BIRTH SMALLINT
                         CHECK(YEAR_OF_BIRTH < 1988),
           SEX           CHAR(1)
                         NOT NULL
                         CHECK(SEX IN ('M','F')),
           YEAR_JOINED   SMALLINT
                         NOT NULL
                         CHECK(YEAR_JOINED > 1950),
           STREET        CHAR(15)
                         NOT NULL,
           HOUSENO       CHAR(4),
           POSTCODE      CHAR(6),
           TOWN          CHAR(10)
                         NOT NULL,
           PHONENO       CHAR(10),
           LEAGUENO      CHAR(4),
           UNIQUE        (NAME, INITIALS),
           CHECK         (YEAR_OF_BIRTH < YEAR_JOINED))


CREATE    TABLE TEAMS
          (TEAMNO        SMALLINT
                         NOT NULL
                         PRIMARY KEY
                         CHECK(TEAMNO BETWEEN 1 AND 10),
           PLAYERNO      SMALLINT
                         NOT NULL
                         REFERENCES PLAYERS(PLAYERNO),
           DIVISION      CHAR(6)
                         NOT NULL)
```

```
CREATE    TABLE GAMES
          (TEAMNO        SMALLINT
                         NOT NULL
                         REFERENCES TEAMS(TEAMNO),
          PLAYERNO       SMALLINT
                         NOT NULL
                         REFERENCES PLAYERS(PLAYERNO),
          WON            SMALLINT
                         NOT NULL
                         DEFAULT 0,
          LOST           SMALLINT
                         NOT NULL
                         DEFAULT 0,
          PRIMARY KEY    (TEAMNO, PLAYERNO),
          CHECK          (WON + LOST < 50))


CREATE    TABLE PENALTIES
          (PAYMENTNO     INTEGER
                         NOT NULL
                         PRIMARY KEY,
          PLAYERNO       SMALLINT
                         NOT NULL
                         REFERENCES GAMES(PLAYERNO),
          DATE           CHAR(6)
                         NOT NULL,
          AMOUNT         DECIMAL(7,2)
                         NOT NULL)
```

7.2 GRANT

Description

The GRANT statement (or <privilege definition>) is used to give users privileges. A privilege is always granted for a particular table. SQL recognizes the following privileges:

- SELECT: privilege to query a table
- INSERT: privilege to add new rows to a table
- UPDATE: privilege to change values in a table
- DELETE: privilege to remove rows from a table
- REFERENCES: privilege to specify columns in a table by defining them as a foreign key.

Format

```
<privilege definition> ::=
   GRANT <privileges>
   ON     <table name>
   TO     <grantees>
   [ WITH GRANT OPTION ]

<privileges> ::=
   ALL PRIVILEGES | <action> [ {,<action>}... ]

<action> ::=
   SELECT |
   INSERT |
   DELETE |
   UPDATE <column list> |
   REFERENCES <column list>

<column list> ::= ( [ <column name> [ {,<column name>}... ] ] )

<table name> ::=
   [ <authorization identifier>. ] <table identifier>

<grantees> ::=
   PUBLIC |
   <authorization identifier>
      [ {,<authorization identifier>}... ]
```

Additional rules

1. Each column name for which the UPDATE or REFERENCES privilege is specified must belong to the table on which the privileges have been granted.

2. ALL PRIVILEGE is equivalent to the summation of the privileges SELECT, INSERT, DELETE, UPDATE (on all columns) and REFERENCES (on all columns).

3. When the UPDATE privilege omits column names the implication is that all columns in the table can be updated.

4. The INSERT, UPDATE and DELETE privileges can only be granted for an updatable table.

Examples

Give JANE the SELECT privilege for the PLAYERS table.

```
GRANT    SELECT
ON       PLAYERS
TO       JANE
```

Give PETE the UPDATE privilege for the PLAYERNO and DIVISION columns of the TEAMS table:

```
GRANT    UPDATE (PLAYERNO, DIVISION)
ON       TEAMS
TO       PETE
```

Give JOHN the INSERT and UPDATE privileges (for all columns) for the TEAMS table, which he can pass on to other users:

```
GRANT    INSERT, UPDATE
ON       TEAMS
TO       JOHN
WITH     GRANT OPTION
```

Give every user the SELECT privilege on the TEAMS table.

```
GRANT    SELECT
ON       TEAMS
TO       PUBLIC
```

Give BEN the privilege to specify foreign keys for his own tables which refer to PLAYERNO column in the PLAYERS table.

```
GRANT    REFERENCES(PLAYERNO)
ON       PLAYERS
TO       BEN
```

BEN may now create the following table:

```
CREATE   TABLE CHILDREN
         (NAME          CHAR(10)
                        NOT NULL,
          PLAYERNO      SMALLINT
                        REFERENCES PLAYERS(PLAYERNO),
          PRIMARY KEY   (NAME, PLAYERNO))
```

Chapter 8

Definitions of additional SQL statements

In this chapter we describe SQL statements which *do not appear in the ISO standard*, but are implemented by many suppliers of SQL.

- ALTER TABLE
- COMMENT
- CREATE INDEX
- CREATE SYNONYM
- DROP INDEX
- DROP SYNONYM
- DROP TABLE
- DROP VIEW
- LOCK
- REVOKE

A number of statements from this list will be included in the SQL standard. As in Chapter 4, we give for each statement:

- a description (what the statement does)
- the format; sometimes we also repeat definitions of the common elements in order to clarify the syntax
- additional rules which are not included in the BNF, but are concerned with the syntax of SQL
- general rules which have to do with the meaning of statements
- examples

We present the statements in alphabetical order.

8.1 ALTER TABLE

Description

The ALTER TABLE statement is used to add and delete columns to and from an existing table.

Format

```
<alter table definition> ::=
    ALTER TABLE <table name> <alter action>

<table name> ::=
    [ <authorization identifier>. ] <table identifier>

<alter action> ::=
    ADD <column name> <data type> |
    DROP <column name>

<data type> ::=
    CHARACTER [ ( <length> ) ] |
    CHAR      [ ( <length> ) ] |
    NUMERIC   [ ( <precision> [,<scale>] ) ] |
    DECIMAL   [ ( <precision> [,<scale>] ) ] |
    DEC       [ ( <precision> [,<scale>] ) ] |
    INTEGER   |
    INT       |
    SMALLINT  |
    FLOAT     [ ( <precision> ) ] |
    REAL      |
    DOUBLE PRECISION
```

Additional rules

1. The name of a new column which is added to a table may not have already been used in the set of column names for that table.

2. A column may only be removed if it exists and is not the only column.

3. No new column may be defined NOT NULL.

General rules

1.   When a column is added to a table which already contains some rows of
     data, the new column is filled with NULL values.

Examples

The TEAMS table needs an extra column called TYPE. This column identifies
whether a team is a men's or women's team.

```
ALTER     TABLE TEAMS
ADD       TYPE  CHAR(1)
```

The TEAMS table now looks like this (the TYPE column is filled with NULL
values in every row):

```
TEAMNO  PLAYERNO  DIVISION  TYPE
------  --------  --------  ----
     1         6  first     ?
     2        27  second    ?
```

Delete the TOWN column from the PLAYERS table:

```
ALTER TABLE PLAYERS DROP TOWN
```

8.2 COMMENT

Description

The COMMENT statement is used to enter a description for tables and columns.

Format

```
<comment definition> ::=
   COMMENT ON <comment specification>
   IS <character string literal>

<comment specification> ::=
   TABLE <table name> |
   COLUMN <table name>.<column name>

<table name> ::=
   [ <authorization identifier>. ] <table identifier>
```

Additional rules

1. The maximum length of the comment is dependent on the supplier.

Examples

Add comment to the PLAYERS table.

```
COMMENT ON
TABLE   PLAYERS
IS      'Recreation and competition players'
```

Add comment to the PLAYERNO column in the PLAYERS table.

```
COMMENT ON
COLUMN  PLAYERS.PLAYERNO
IS      'Primary key'
```

8.3 CREATE INDEX

Description

The CREATE INDEX statement is used to define an alternative, direct access to data via one or more columns in the table. At the same time a unique constraint definition can be defined using an index.

Note: An index is *not* a logical database structure and therefore does not appear in the SQL standard, nor will it be included in the SQL2 standard.

Format

```
<index definition> ::=
   CREATE [ UNIQUE ] INDEX <index name>
   ON     <table name>
   ( <index column> [ {,<index column>}... ] )

<table name> ::=
   [ <authorization identifier>. ] <table identifier>

<index column> ::=
   <column name> [ ASC | DESC ]
```

Additional rules

1.   Two indexes may not have the same name.

General rules

1.   An index can be defined on a table which is either empty or already contains rows.

2.   By adding ASC or DESC the index is built in ascending or descending order respectively.

3.   When neither ASC nor DESC is specified, the index is built in ascending order.

4.   By adding the word 'UNIQUE' a unique constraint definition can be specified.

Examples

Create an index on the POSTCODE column in the PLAYERS table.

```
CREATE INDEX PLAY_PC
ON     PLAYERS (POSTCODE)
```

Create an index on the combination of columns WON and LOST in the
GAMES table.

```
CREATE INDEX GAM_WL
ON     GAMES (WON, LOST)
```

Create a *unique* index on the PLAYERNO column in the PLAYERS table.

```
CREATE UNIQUE INDEX PRIM_KEY
ON     PLAYERS(PLAYERNO)
```

8.4   CREATE SYNONYM

Description

The CREATE SYNONYM statement is used to define a synonym for a table name. Synonyms can be used for example in SELECT and UPDATE statements instead of using table names.

Format

```
<synonym definition> ::=
   CREATE SYNONYM <table identifier>
   FOR <table name>

<table name> ::=
   [ <authorization identifier>. ] <table identifier>
```

Additional rules

1.   A user may not create two synonyms with the same name.

Examples

Pete defines a synonym for the PLAYERS table which has been created by Diane.

```
CREATE SYNONYM PLA
FOR     DIANE.PLAYERS
```

Pete can now access the table in the following way:

```
SELECT  *
FROM    PLA
```

8.5 DROP INDEX

Description

The DROP INDEX statement is used to remove an index from a table.

Format

```
<drop index definition> ::=
   DROP INDEX <index name>
```

Examples

Delete the index PLAY_PC.

```
DROP INDEX PLAY_PC
```

8.6 DROP SYNONYM

Description

The DROP SYNONYM statement is used to delete synonyms.

Format

```
<drop synonym definition> ::=
   DROP SYNONYM <table name>

<table name> ::=
   [ <authorization identifier>. ] <table identifier>
```

Examples

Delete synonym PLA.

```
DROP SYNONYM PLA
```

8.7 DROP TABLE

Description

The DROP TABLE statement is used to delete tables in their entirety.

Format

```
<drop table definition> ::=
    DROP TABLE <table name>

<table name> ::=
    [ <authorization identifier>. ] <table identifier>
```

General rules

1. All views, synonyms and privileges based on this table are also deleted.

Examples

Delete the PLAYERS table.

```
DROP TABLE PLAYERS
```

8.8 DROP VIEW

Description

Views are deleted using the DROP VIEW statement.

Format

```
<drop view definition> ::=
   DROP VIEW <table name>

<table name> ::=
   [ <authorization identifier>. ] <table identifier>
```

General rules

1. Every other view which refers to the deleted view is also deleted. The
    automatic deletion of these views can lead, of course, to the deletion of
    still more views.

Examples

Delete the PLAYERS_PER_TEAM view.

```
DROP VIEW PLAYERS_PER_TEAM
```

8.9 LOCK

Description

The LOCK statement is used to lock an entire table. Other users or programs can then either not access the table at all or can only read the contents of the table.

Format

```
<lock statement> ::=
    LOCK TABLE <table name>
        IN { SHARE | EXCLUSIVE } MODE

<table name> ::=
    [ <authorization identifier>. ] <table identifier>
```

General rules

1.   SHARE means that other users can query the table.

2.   EXCLUSIVE means that the table is totally inaccessible to other programs.

3.   The lock which is set up by the LOCK statement remains in force until a subsequent COMMIT or ROLLBACK statement is issued or until the end of the program.

8.10 REVOKE

Description

The REVOKE statement is used to withdraw privileges which have been granted by the GRANT statement.

Format

```
<revoke definition> ::=
   REVOKE  <privileges>
   ON      <table name>
   FROM    <grantees>

<privileges> ::=
   ALL PRIVILEGES |
   <action> [ {,<action>}... ]

<action> ::=
   SELECT |
   INSERT |
   DELETE |
   UPDATE ( <column list> )

<column list> ::=
   ( <column name> [ ,{<column name>}... ] )

<table name> ::=
   [ <authorization identifier>. ] <table identifier>

<grantees> ::=
   PUBLIC |
   <authorization identifier>
      [ {,<authorization identifier>}... ]
```

Additional rules

1. All privileges which are directly or indirectly dependent on a particular privilege are deleted when that privilege is withdrawn.

2. Tables and views created by someone whose privileges have been revoked remain.

Examples

Revoke the SELECT privilege on the PLAYERS table from John.

```
REVOKE    SELECT
ON        PLAYERS
FROM      JOHN
```

Appendix A

Reserved words

The SQL standard (level 2) recognizes the following reserved words:

```
ALL, AND, ANY, AS, ASC, AUTHORIZATION, AVG,
BEGIN, BETWEEN, BY,
CHAR, CHARACTER, CHECK, CLOSE, COBOL, COMMIT,
CONTINUE, COUNT, CREATE, CURRENT, CURSOR,
DEC, DECIMAL, DECLARE, DELETE, DESC, DISTINCT, DOUBLE,
END, ESCAPE, EXEC, EXISTS,
FETCH, FLOAT, FOR, FORTRAN, FOUND, FROM,
GO, GOTO, GRANT, GROUP,
HAVING,
IN, INDICATOR, INSERT, INT, INTEGER, INTO, IS,
LANGUAGE, LIKE,
MAX, MIN, MODULE, NOT, NULL, NUMERIC,
OF, ON, OPEN, OPTION, OR, ORDER,
PASCAL, PLI, PRECISION, PRIVILEGES, PROCEDURE, PUBLIC,
REAL, ROLLBACK,
SCHEMA, SECTION, SELECT, SET, SMALLINT, SOME,
SQL, SQLCODE, SQLERROR, SUM,
TABLE, TO,
UNION, UNIQUE, UPDATE, USER,
VALUES, VIEW,
WHENEVER, WHERE, WITH, WORK
```

The following reserved words have been added in Addendum 1:

```
DEFAULT,
FOREIGN,
KEY,
PRIMARY,
REFERENCES
```

Appendix B

SQL Syntax

B.1 Data Definition Language

```
<schema> ::=
   CREATE SCHEMA AUTHORIZATION <authorization identifier>
   [ <schema element>... ]

        <schema element> ::=
           <table definition> |
           <view definition> |
           <privilege definition>

<table definition> ::=
   CREATE TABLE <table name>
   ( <table element> [ {,<table element>}... ] )

        <table element> ::=
           <column definition> |
           <unique constraint definition>

        <column definition> ::=
           <column name> <data type> [ NOT NULL [ UNIQUE ] ]

        <unique constraint definition> ::=
           UNIQUE <column list>

<view definition> ::=
   CREATE VIEW <table name>
      [ <column list> ]
      AS <query specification>
      [ WITH CHECK OPTION ]

<privilege definition> ::=
   GRANT <privileges>
   ON    <table name>
   TO    <grantees>
   [ WITH GRANT OPTION ]
```

B.2 Module Language

```
<module> ::=
    MODULE         [ <module name> ]
    LANGUAGE       <programming language>
    AUTHORIZATION  <authorization identifier>
    [ <declare cursor>... ]
    <procedure>...


<procedure> ::=
    PROCEDURE <procedure name> <parameter declaration>...;
    <sql statement>


        <sql statement> ::=
            <close statement>    |
            <commit statement>   |
            <delete statement>   |
            <fetch statement>    |
            <insert statement>   |
            <open statement>     |
            <rollback statement> |
            <select statement>   |
            <update statement>
```

B.3 Data Manipulation Language

```
<close statement> ::=
    CLOSE <cursor name>


<commit statement> ::=
    COMMIT WORK


<declare cursor> ::=
    DECLARE <cursor name> CURSOR FOR
    <query expression>
    [ <order by clause> ]


        <order by clause> ::=
            ORDER BY <sort specification>
                    [ {,<sort specification>}... ]


        <sort specification> ::=
            { <sequence number> | <column specification> } [ ASC | DESC ]


<delete statement> ::=
    DELETE FROM <table name>
    [ WHERE { CURRENT OF <cursor name> | <search condition> } ]
```

```
<embedded exception condition> ::=
    WHENEVER <condition> <exception action>


        <condition> ::=
            SQLERROR | NOT FOUND


        <exception action> ::=
            CONTINUE    |
            GOTO <target> |
            GO TO <target>


<fetch statement> ::=
    FETCH <cursor name>
    INTO <target specification> [ {,<target specification>}... ]


<insert statement> ::=
    INSERT INTO <table name>
    [ <column list> ]
    { VALUES ( <value> {,<value>}... ) | <query specification> }


        <value> ::=
            <value specification> | NULL


<open statement> ::=
    OPEN <cursor name>


<rollback statement> ::=
    ROLLBACK WORK


<select statement> ::=
    SELECT [ ALL | DISTINCT ] <select list>
    INTO   <target specification>
           [ {,<target specification>}... ]
    <table expression>


<update statement> ::=
    UPDATE <table name>
    SET    <object column> [ {,<object column>}... ]
    [ WHERE { CURRENT OF <cursor name> | <search condition> } ]


        <object column> ::=
            <column name> = { <value expression> | NULL }
```

B.4 Common Elements

```
<action> ::=
    SELECT |
    INSERT |
    DELETE |
    UPDATE <column list>


<all set function> ::=
    { AVG | MAX | MIN | SUM } ( [ ALL ] <value expression> )


<approximate numeric literal> ::= <mantissa>E<exponent>


<authorization identifier> ::= <identifier>


<boolean factor> ::= [ NOT ] <boolean primary>


<boolean primary> ::=
    <predicate> | ( <search condition> )


<boolean term> ::=
    <boolean factor> |
    <boolean term> AND <boolean factor>


<character> ::= <digit> | <letter> | <special character>


<character representation> ::= <nonquote character> | ''


<character string literal> ::= '<character representation>...'


<column list> ::= ( <column name> [ {,<column name>}... ] )


<column name> ::= <identifier>


<column specification> ::=
    <column name> |
    <table name>.<column name> |
    <correlation name>.<column name>


<comparison operator> ::= = | <> | < | > | <= | >=


<correlation name> ::= <identifier>


<cursor name> ::= <identifier>
```

```
<data type> ::=
   CHARACTER [ ( <length> ) ] |
   CHAR      [ ( <length> ) ] |
   NUMERIC   [ ( <precision> [,<scale>] ) ] |
   DECIMAL   [ ( <precision> [,<scale>] ) ] |
   DEC       [ ( <precision> [,<scale>] ) ] |
   INTEGER   |
   INT       |
   SMALLINT  |
   FLOAT     [ ( <precision> ) ] |
   REAL      |
   DOUBLE PRECISION


<digit> ::=
   0 | 1 | 2 | 3 | 4 | 5 | 6 | 7 | 8 | 9


<distinct set function> ::=
   { AVG | MAX | MIN | SUM | COUNT }
      ( DISTINCT <column specification> )


<escape character> ::= <value specification>


<exact numeric literal> ::=
   [ + | - ] <unsigned integer> [ .<unsigned integer> ] |
   [ + | - ] <unsigned integer>. |
   [ + | - ] .<unsigned integer>


<exponent> ::= [ + | - ] <digit>...


<factor> ::=
   [ + | - ] <primary>


<from clause> ::=
   FROM <table reference> [ {,<table reference>}... ]


      <grantees> ::=
         PUBLIC |
         <authorization identifier> [ {,<authorization identifier>}... ]


<group by clause> ::=
   GROUP BY <column specification> [ {,<column specification>}... ]


<having clause> ::=
   HAVING <search condition>


<identifier> ::= <upper case letter>
   [ { [ _ ] { <upper case letter> | <digit> } }... ]
```

```
<length> ::= <unsigned integer>


<letter> ::=
   <lower case letter> | <upper case letter>


<literal> ::=
   <character string literal> |
   <numeric literal>


<lower case letter> ::=
   a | b | c | d | e | f | g | h | i | j |
   k | l | m | n | o | p | q | r | s | t |
   u | v | w | x | y | z


<mantissa> ::= <exact numeric literal>


<module name> ::= <identifier>


<numeric literal> ::=
   <exact numeric literal> | <approximate numeric literal>


<parameter name> ::= <identifier>


   <parameter declaration> ::=
      <parameter name> <data type> | SQLCODE


<parameter specification> ::=
   <parameter name> [ [ INDICATOR ] <parameter name> ]


<pattern> ::= <value specification>


<precision> ::= <unsigned integer>


<predicate> ::=
   <value expression> <comparison operator> <value expression> |
   <value expression> <comparison operator> <subquery> |
   <value expression> [ NOT ] BETWEEN <value expression>
      AND <value expression> |
   <value expression> [ NOT ] IN
      ( <value specification> {,<value specification>}... ) |
   <value expression> [ NOT ] IN <subquery> |
   <column specification> [ NOT ] LIKE <pattern>
      [ ESCAPE <escape-character> ] |
   <column specification> IS [ NOT ] NULL |
   <value expression> <comparison operator> ALL <subquery> |
   <value expression> <comparison operator> ANY <subquery> |
   <value expression> <comparison operator> SOME <subquery> |
   EXISTS <subquery>
```

```
<primary> ::=
   <value specification> |
   <column specification> |
   <set function specification> |
   ( <value expression> )


      <privileges> ::=
          ALL PRIVILEGES |
          <action> [ {,<action>}... ]


<procedure name> ::= <identifier>


      <programming language> ::=
          COBOL | FORTRAN | PASCAL | PLI


<query expression> ::=
   <query term> |
   <query expression> UNION [ ALL ] <query term>


<query specification> ::=
   SELECT [ ALL | DISTINCT ] <select list>
   <table expression>


<query term> ::=
   <query specification> | ( <query expression> )


<scale> ::= <unsigned integer>


<search condition> ::=
   <boolean term> |
   <search condition> OR <boolean term>


<select list> ::=
   <value expression> [ {,<value expression>}... ] | *


      <sequence number> ::= <unsigned integer>


<set function specification> ::=
   COUNT(*) |
   <distinct set function> |
   <all set function>


<subquery> ::=
   ( SELECT [ ALL | DISTINCT ] { <value expression> | * }
   <table expression> )


<system variable> ::= USER
```

```
<table expression> ::=
   <from clause>
   [ <where clause> ]
   [ <group by clause> ]
   [ <having clause> ]


<table identifier> ::= <identifier>


<table name> ::=
   [ <authorization identifier>. ] <table identifier>


<table reference> ::=
   <table name> [ <correlation name> ]


<target specification> ::=
   <parameter specification> |
   <variable specification>


<term> ::=
   <factor> |
   <term> * <factor> |
   <term> / <factor>


<unsigned integer> ::= <digit>...


<upper case letter> ::=
   A | B | C | D | E | F | G | H | I | J |
   K | L | M | N | O | P | Q | R | S | T |
   U | V | W | X | Y | Z


<value expression> ::=
   <term> |
   <value expression> + <term> |
   <value expression> - <term>


<value specification> ::=
   <parameter specification> |
   <variable specification> |
   <literal> |
   <system variable>


<variable specification> ::=
   <variable name> [ [ INDICATOR ] <variable name> ]


<where clause> ::=
   WHERE <search condition>
```

---

132   B · SQL SYNTAX

B.5 Additional SQL statements

```
<alter table definition> ::=
   ALTER TABLE <table name> <alter action>


        <alter action> ::=
            ADD <column name> <data type> |
            DROP <column name>


<comment definition> ::=
   COMMENT ON <comment specification>
   IS <character string literal>


        <comment specification> ::=
            TABLE <table name> |
            COLUMN <table name>.<column name>


<index definition> ::=
   CREATE [ UNIQUE ] INDEX <index name>
   ON      <table name>
   ( <index column> [ {,<index column>}... ] )


        <index column> ::=
            <column name> [ ASC | DESC ]


<synonym definition> ::=
   CREATE SYNONYM <table identifier>
   FOR <table name>


<drop index definition> ::=
   DROP INDEX <index name>


<drop synonym definition> ::=
   DROP SYNONYM <table name>


<drop table definition> ::=
   DROP TABLE <table name>


<drop view statement> ::=
   DROP VIEW <table name>


<lock statement> ::=
   LOCK TABLE <table name>
      IN { SHARE | EXCLUSIVE } MODE


<revoke definition> ::=
   REVOKE <privileges>
   ON      <table name>
   FROM    <grantees>
```

Appendix C

References

[DATE87] C.J. Date, 'A Guide to The SQL Standard', Addison-Wesley Publishing Company, 1987.

[ISO87a] ISO TC97/SC21/WG3 and ANSI X3H2, 'ISO 9075 Database Language SQL', 1987.

[ISO87b] ISO TC97/SC21/WG3 and ANSI X3H2, 'ISO 9075 Database Language SQL Addendum 1 Integrity Enhancements', 1987.

[ISO88] ISO DBL SYD-2 and ANSI X3H2-88-259, 'ISO-ANSI (working draft) Database Language SQL2', July 1988.

[LANS88] R.F. van der Lans, 'Introduction to SQL', Addison-Wesley Publishing Company, 1988.

[SCHM83] J.W. Schmidt and M.L. Brodie, 'Relational Database Systems: Analysis and Comparison', Springer-Verlag, 1983.

Index

A

action 70, 106, 121
addendum 123
adding columns 110
adding rows 73
ALL 25, 30, 32, 36, 38, 41, 84
ALL PRIVILEGES 70, 106
all set function 38
alter action 110
ALTER TABLE statement 110
AND 25, 36
ANSI 1
ANY 25, 36
ASC
    in index 113
    in ordering 63
authorization identifier 24, 46, 70
AVG 38

B

base table 57
BEGIN DECLARE SECTION 90
BETWEEN 25, 36
BNF notation 6
boolean 25, 36
    — factor 36
    — primary 36
    — term 36

C

CHARACTER 20
character 18
    — representation 22
    — string literal 22
CHECK 100
check constraint definition 100
CLOSE statement 52
COBOL 76, 89, 91

cobol
    — data type 91
    — variable definition 91
column
    — constraint definition 100
    — definition 57, 100
    — list 57, 60, 70, 73, 100, 106, 121
    — name 19, 24
    — specification 19, 47
COMMENT statement 112
commit point 53
COMMIT statement 53, 83
comparison operator 25, 97
concurrency 53
condition 93
conformance 6
constraint definition 100
CONTINUE 93
correlation name 19, 24
COUNT 38
CREATE INDEX statement 113
CREATE SCHEMA statement 55
CREATE SYNONYM statement 115
CREATE TABLE statement 57, 100
CREATE VIEW statement 60
CURRENT OF 66, 86, 98
cursor 3, 52, 63, 66, 68, 79, 86
cursor name 24, 63

D

Data Definition Language (DDL) 2
Data Manipulation Language (DML) 2, 3
data type 20, 57, 80, 100, 110
database 3
Date C.J. 5
DDL statement 2
DECIMAL 20

declaration of variables 91
declare cursor 76
DECLARE SECTION 90
DECLARE statement 52, 63, 79
DEFAULT value 100
DELETE statement 66
deleting columns 110
deleting rows 66
DESC (index) 113
DESC (ordering) 63
digit 18, 22
DISTINCT 30, 32, 38, 41, 60, 73, 84
distinct set function 38
DML statement 3
DOUBLE PRECISION 20, 98
DROP INDEX statement 116
DROP SYNONYM statement 117
DROP TABLE statement 118
DROP VIEW statement 119

E

embedded exception declaration 92
embedded SQL 2, 4, 89
    prefix 90
END DECLARE SECTION 90
END-EXEC 90
escape character 25
exact numeric literal 22
exception action 93
EXCLUSIVE 120
EXEC SQL 90
EXISTS 25, 36, 97
exponent 22

F

factor 47
FETCH statement 68, 79
FLOAT 20
foreign key 100
FORTRAN 76, 89, 91
    example program 94
fortran variable definition 91
from clause 32, 41, 44

function 38

G

GAMES table 11
GOTO 93
GRANT statement 70, 106
grantee 70, 106, 121
granting privileges 70
group by clause 32, 41, 44

H

having clause 32, 41, 44
host language 89

I

IBM 1
identifier 24
IN 25, 36
index 113, 116
    — column 113
    — definition 113
indicating SQL statements 90
INDICATOR 49, 68, 84
INSERT statement 73
INTEGER 20
integrity rule 2, 57
INTO 84
invoking procedures 4

L

length
    — of data types 20
    — of identifiers 97
letter 18
LIKE 25, 36, 97
literal 22, 49
    character string — 22
    numeric — 22
LOCK statement 120
lower case letter 18

M

mantissa 22
MAX 38
metasymbol 6
MIN 38
module 4
    — name 24
Module Language 2, 4
MODULE statement 76

N

name 24
    length of — 24
nines 91
non-terminal symbol 6
NOT 25, 36
NOT FOUND 93
NOT NULL 57, 98, 100
NULL
    — in search condition 25, 36
    — in UPDATE statement 86
NULL value 38, 73, 97
NUMERIC 20, 98

O

object column 86
OPEN statement 52, 79
OR 25, 36
ORDER BY 63, 98
order by clause 63
owner of schema 55

P

parameter 98
    — declaration 80
    — name 24
    — specification 49, 68, 84
PASCAL 76
Pascal 89, 91
    example program 95
pascal variable definition 91
pattern 25, 36
PENALTIES table 11

PL/I 76, 89, 91
pl1 data type 91
pl1 variable definition 91
PLAYERS table 11
precision 20
predicate 25, 36
prefix (embedded SQL) 100
primary 47
primary key 100
priorities of operators for calcula-
    tions 48
privilege 70, 106, 121
    — definition 106, 70
procedure 4, 76, 80
    — name 24
production rule 6
programming language 76
PUBLIC 70, 106, 121

Q

query
    — expression 30, 63
    — specification 30, 32, 60, 73
    — term 30
quotation mark 22

R

REAL 20, 98
recovery 53
REFERENCES 100, 106
referential constraint definition 100
reserved words 123
REVOKE statement 121
ROLLBACK statement 53, 83

S

sample database 15
    — contents 15
    — description 9
    — schema 13
    — structure 12
scale 20
schema 3, 55, 97

schema element 55
search condition 25, 36
SELECT 30, 32, 41
select list 30, 32, 60, 73, 84
SELECT statement 84
sequence number (ordering) 63
set function 97
    — specification 38, 47
SHARE 120
SMALLINT 20
SOME 25, 36
sort specification 63
special character 18
sports club 9
SQL standard 1
    addendum 1, 5, 99
    history of — 1
    levels 5, 97
sql statement 80
SQL2 (standard) 2, 3
SQLCOD (FORTRAN) 90
SQLCODE 80, 89, 93, 98
SQLERROR 93
subquery 36, 41
substitution rule 6
SUM 38
symbol 6
synonym 115, 117
synonym definition 115
system variable 49

T

table 57, 110, 112, 115, 117, 118
    base — 57
    — constraint definition 100
    creation of — 57
    — definition 57, 100
    — element 57, 100
    — expression 30, 32, 41, 44, 60,
        73, 84
    — identifier 24, 46
    — name 19, 46, 57, 60, 66, 70,
        73, 86, 100, 110
    — reference 32, 41, 44
    — specification 106

virtual — 60
target
    in WHENEVER statement 93
    — specification 68, 84
TC97/SC21/WG3 1
TEAMS table 11
term 47
terminal symbol 6
transaction 53, 83, 98
truth table 37

U

UNION 30, 98
UNIQUE 57, 97, 100, 113
unique constraint definition 57, 97,
    100
unsigned integer 22
UPDATE statement 86
upper case letter 18
USER 49, 97
user 55

V

value 73
    — expression 41, 47, 84
    — specification 47, 49
VALUES 73
variable specification 49, 68, 84
view 60, 119
    creation of — 60
    — definition 60
virtual table 60

W

WHENEVER statement 92
where clause 32, 41, 44
WITH CHECK OPTION 60, 98
WITH GRANT OPTION 70, 98,
    106
WORK 53, 83